LEADING
SMALL GROUPS

LEADING SMALL GROUPS

HOW TO GATHER, LAUNCH, LEAD,

AND MULTIPLY YOUR SMALL GROUP

CHRIS SURRATT

B&H
PUBLISHING GROUP

NASHVILLE, TENNESSEE

978-1-5359-3469-5

Published by B&H Publishing Group
Nashville, Tennessee

Dewey Decimal Classification: 268.3
Subject Heading: BIBLE—STUDY AND TEACHING
/ RELIGIOUS EDUCATION / SMALL GROUPS—
RELIGIOUS ASPECTS

Cover design and illustration by Matt Lehman.

3 4 5 6 7 8 9 • 23 22 21 20 19

Contents

Section IV: Multiplying Your Small Group

Foreword

t's an honor to endorse and write this foreword for Chris Surratt's latest book, *Leading Small Groups*. I owe my faith to a small group. I grew up in a nominally Catholic home but did not respond to the good news of the gospel until my sister brought it home with her from a small group. A friend of hers had bravely decided to start the group and invited my sister to be part of it. Through that group my sister became a follower of Christ. When she shared her experience with me, I, too, put my faith in Jesus. My parents also became Christians all because of the influence of that one small group. Later, my three older brothers and their wives and kids followed. The group that my sister's friend started changed the destiny of our entire family—nineteen people!

What is especially remarkable and special to me about that group is that my sister's friend was not a religious professional. She had not received special training. She was just an ordinary follower of Christ who answered the call to start a small group. Her willingness to step out and lead a group had eternal consequences on my family, as well as on people to whom my family and I have ministered since. Is it any wonder that I have devoted most of the last thirty years of my life to small groups? A small group changed my life! Over the years, I've had the privilege of seeing the profound effects small groups have had on the lives of literally tens of thousands of other people.

The reason that small groups are so effective is that they are part of God's plan for His church. From the moment the church was born and three thousand people responded to Peter's message on the day of Pentecost, small groups have been part of God's primary strategy. The early church met in the temple courts for large group worship and in homes for small group fellowship. Both meetings had equal importance. Later, when persecution made meetings in the temple courts impossible, the church continued to meet and grow through small groups. Through the centuries, whenever public worship has been banned, the church has continued to meet in small groups and flourish despite the oppression. History has proven that the church can survive and even continue to grow without large group worship when it has a healthy system of small groups.

Small groups are so potent and resilient because of the commitment and courage of seemingly ordinary followers of Christ, like my sister's friend, who step up to lead them. If you are reading this, you probably have already decided to become one of those people. Let me be among the first to thank you and encourage you as you take this exciting step in your faith journey. You've already done the hard part. You've made the decision. Now that you have this book by Chris, you will gain much of the information and insights you'll need to lead your group well.

Chris has synthesized his years of experience as a small group leader, pastor, and expert into this valuable resource. You'll find his insights both helpful and practical. He'll provide you with a scriptural framework for small groups as well as offer down-to-earth advice on how to make your group a success. He'll give you everything you'll need from gathering your group to getting it started to leading it well, and even how to multiply your leadership by starting more groups. I'd suggest soaking up all you can from this book with your first reading, then using it as a reference going forward. You'll undoubtedly run into challenges along the way as you lead your group—anything worthwhile comes with challenges—and Chris's book will provide you with excellent direction on how to negotiate them effectively.

Congratulations again on your decision to lead and use this book by Chris to help change people's destiny. Enjoy the adventure!

Steve Gladen
Pastor of Small Groups, Saddleback Church
Author, *Leading Small Groups with Purpose*

Introduction

still remember when my wife and I were approached about the possibility of leading our first small group. My experience with church groups before this was in Sunday school, with different age groups meeting on the church campus before the Sunday morning service. Our current church had small groups that met in homes around the city. Although we had been attending a small group for a short time, the thought of leading one wasn't on the radar.

I am an introvert by nature, so the thought of inviting a group of people into our home every week so we could "do life together" was not appealing. Plus, we were newly married, and the group we were tasked with leading was a Young Marrieds group. How on earth were we going to help other couples be better spouses and parents when we didn't have a clue ourselves?

All the normal insecurities and doubts told me to say "no."

- I don't have it all together enough to lead anyone.

- I don't know enough about the Bible to lead a Bible study.
- Our tiny house couldn't fit everyone.
- I don't have enough time for something else every week.
- Will I have to be friends with everyone in the group?

With some hesitation and encouragement from my more extroverted (and friendly) wife, Jenny, we said "yes" to leading our first small group. Twenty years and counting, in three cities and six different living rooms, we're still at it.

I cannot imagine what life would have been like without those first couples coming alongside us through the joy and tears of life. I can say now: we did and are still doing life together with the people in our small groups.

If you are reading this and thinking the same thoughts I was about the potential of being a small group leader, you are in the perfect spot. Your small group doesn't need a leader who has it all figured out. They don't need a leader who has the perfect marriage, house, kids, pets, and cookware. They don't need a leader with a seminary degree (although it's not a bad thing if you happen to have one). Your small group needs a leader willing to say, "I'm messed up too; let's figure this thing out together."

One of my favorite quotes is from C. S. Lewis, who defined friendship this way: "The typical expression of opening Friendship would be something like, 'What? You too? I thought I was the only one.'"[1]

A small group experience is a series of "You too?" moments. Every one of us is messed up and in need of a risen Savior and a group of people to hold on to when the waters get rough. Even us introverts. We may not show it a lot, but we need people to walk alongside as much as anyone else. We just may not need as *many* people as extroverts do.

This book is written and designed to take you through the journey of building your own small group. That group could be in your home, a neighborhood clubhouse, a break room at work, or a classroom at the church. The location does not matter; what matters is what takes place inside it.

There will be practical tips you can use immediately as you start your new small group or look to make your current group experience better. Every chapter will end with a set of questions to answer as you work through that step of the journey. I would suggest returning to this book as you walk through the different stages of your small group. There are a few things you will need to know from the beginning, and the rest will become more necessary while "on the job."

We are all in this together. Please know all of your fellow small group leaders are cheering you on. Let's go change the world one small group at a time!

QUESTIONS TO THINK ABOUT

1. Why do you want to lead a small group?

_____

_____

2. What is your experience with small groups?

_____

_____

3. What are your biggest doubts about leading?

_____

_____

SECTION I

Gathering Your Small Group

CHAPTER 1

What Is a Small Group Leader?

The number-one barrier to someone stepping up to lead a small group is the word *leader*.

Take five seconds right now and think about what you imagine when you hear that word. Go ahead, I'll wait. What came to mind? A CEO of a large company? A head of state? The senior pastor of your church?

We all have preconceived ideas of what a leader should be, sound, and look like. I imagine someone who is tall (I'm short), extroverted (I'm an introvert), a scholar (I, um . . . struggled), and forceful (definitely not me). Basically, someone who is the opposite of me.

There is no template for an effective leader. Every successful leader is flawed. In fact, the Bible is filled with damaged and flawed leaders. Here are just a few:

- Adam, the first human being, couldn't lead his own family. His firstborn ended up killing his brother.
- Eve, the first woman, became greedy and took the first bite (literally) into sin.
- Noah, the last righteous man on Earth at the time, got drunk and slept in the nude (in view of his kids).
- Abraham, the forefather of faith, let other men walk off with his wife on two different occasions.
- Sarah, the wife of Abraham, let her husband sleep with another woman and then hated her for it.
- Moses, the humblest man on the face of the earth, had a serious problem with his temper.
- David, the friend of God, concealed his adultery with a murder.
- Peter, the man Jesus named "the Rock," denied Christ three times.
- Paul, the author of most of the New Testament, was a Pharisee who persecuted Christians before becoming one and was hampered by a "thorn in the flesh" after becoming one.

I could go on and on, but you get the picture: the Bible shows us men and women who had issues just like us. Yet, God still used them to build a movement that has not slowed down in more than two thousand years. Even with the death of the only perfect leader, Jesus!

Michael Kelley says that "Leadership is the joyful acceptance of responsibility at a given moment." I like that definition because, ultimately, leading a small group is supposed to be joyful. It won't always be easy or fun, but knowing you were integral in someone's life being changed through the power of community is one of the most joyful things you will do.

To help us know what a small group leader is, let's consider a few things he or she is not.

- *Someone who has all the answers.* A leader who has all the answers is not a leader anyone should follow. First, it's impossible, but most of all, we want to follow someone humble enough to admit they don't know it all.
- *Someone who can teach the Bible weekly.* There are some with the gift of teaching, but a small group experience is not about one person teaching and the rest learning. It's a shared discussion where we are all growing together. A small group leader is a

facilitator of a synergistic conversation with the Bible as the guide.

- *Someone who is everyone's best friend.* Our job as small group leaders is not to make deep relationships with every person in the group. Not only is that unwise, but it's also unhealthy. Our goal should be to find two to three same-sex people in the group we can disciple outside group time and help other people in the group do the same.

I identify with what Paul said in 1 Corinthians:

I came to you in weakness, in fear, and in much trembling. My speech and my preaching were not with persuasive words of wisdom but with a demonstration of the Spirit's power, so that your faith might not be based on human wisdom but on God's power. (1 Cor. 2:3–5)

Isn't that freeing? God chose me and you, sinners and flawed human beings, because He wants all our faith to be in Him, not in our own abilities. When your group members look at you, they are not putting their faith in you as the leader, but in the Spirit's power working through your weakness.

The Shepherd Leader

Peter gave us this definition of leadership as he exhorted the elders of the first-century church:

> Shepherd God's flock among you, not overseeing out of compulsion but willingly, as God would have you, not out of greed for money but eagerly; not lording it over those entrusted to you, but being examples to the flock. And when the chief Shepherd appears, you will receive the unfading crown of glory. (1 Pet. 5:2–4)

Notice Peter did not say, "Teach God's flock." The spiritual gift of teaching is not the most essential gift for a small group leader. In fact, the teaching gift sometimes does not translate well into leading a small group. That is one reason why a senior pastor is not always a great small group leader. I always suggest a teaching pastor be in a small group but not lead a group.

The elders of the church were put in place to shepherd the congregation in the same way we as small group leaders are to shepherd our portion of the church. Although we are

When your group members look at you, they are not putting their faith in you as the leader, but in the Spirit's power working through your weakness.

not that familiar with shepherds in today's society, God chose shepherds throughout the Bible to lead His people. Abraham, Jacob, Moses, and David were all shepherds chosen as leaders by God. Jesus even referred to Himself as a shepherd: "I am the good shepherd. I know my own, and my own know me" (John 10:14).

Why Did God Choose Shepherds?

Good shepherds lead from the heart. They know each sheep in their care and will work hard to get them to their destination. The small group leader's role is to help the people in their group take the next spiritual step to get them from where they are to where they need to be. A shepherd leader will work hard to make sure no one is left behind on their spiritual journey.

Good shepherds lead with compassion. Jesus (the ultimate shepherd) set the example as a leader who always had compassion for His followers—even when it was most inconvenient.

We see in the book of Matthew Jesus withdrawing for time alone to grieve immediately after receiving the news of the death of John the Baptist, but He still could not escape the crowds.

> When Jesus heard about it, he withdrew from there by boat to a remote place to be alone. When the crowds heard this, they followed him on foot from the towns.

When he went ashore, he saw a large
crowd, had compassion on them, and
healed their sick. (Matt. 14:13–14)

Even though Jesus had every right to not care for
another person at that moment, He saw sheep without
a shepherd and had compassion for them. There will
be many times as a small group leader where a member
of your group will have a need at the most inopportune
moment. It may be a phone call late at night. It may be
someone who wants to stay after group to talk. It may be
someone at church who needs to grab time in the lobby
during the service you are about to attend. While inconvenient, it's at those times where we have to remember
the compassionate example of Jesus.

Good shepherds lead from the front. "When he has
brought all his own outside, he goes ahead of them. The
sheep follow him because they know his voice" (John 10:4).
A leader that people will follow is a leader willing to go first.
This may mean sharing a vulnerable story with the group
to set the example of authenticity. The group will model
the behavior you display. If you want your group to be open,
open your heart first. If you want the group to serve, serve
them first. Leading from the front does not mean dictating
direction. It means setting the example for others to follow.

Good shepherds lead sacrificially. There will be times
when leading your group will be a sacrifice. Jesus said, "I
am the good shepherd. The good shepherd lays down his

life for the sheep" (John 10:11). While your sacrifices will probably not involve laying your life down for someone, opening your home to a group of people weekly is a sacrifice. You have to keep the house clean, put up the pets, pull out all the extra chairs, make sure there is food, etc. It's exhausting to host a group! You will need occasional breaks to not burn out, but that sacrifice of time and effort will lead to a group that bonds through consistency.

At the end of our time as leaders, we want to know we led our flock well. We can look to Jesus, the Good Shepherd, and follow His example of shepherding His flock. Though we will not be perfect, we want to lead from the heart, lead with compassion, lead from the front, and lead sacrificially.

My Experience

There have been countless times over the years when my wife and I have been called on to shepherd the people in our groups through various seasons of life. There have been many baby showers thrown, lots of meals planned during times of need, and several late-night calls from distraught group members. All of those sacrifices have been paid back many times over by our group friends. For example, the time when our moving company cancelled at the last minute, so all of our small group came over within hours to pack a two-story, three-bedroom house into a moving truck until midnight. That's true sacrifice.

QUESTIONS TO THINK ABOUT

1. What stood out to you the most in this chapter?

_____

_____

2. What was your perception of who a leader is before you read this chapter?

_____

_____

3. Which of the shepherd leader qualities (lead from the heart, lead with compassion, lead from the front, lead sacrificially) do you struggle with the most?

_____

_____

4. What steps can you take to become a better shepherd leader?

_____

_____

Creating Biblical Community

The picture of the community we are called to establish with our groups is found in the first-century church.

They devoted themselves to the apostles' teaching, to the fellowship, to the breaking of bread, and to prayer. Everyone was filled with awe, and many wonders and signs were being performed through the apostles. Now all the believers were together and held all things in common. They sold their possessions and property and distributed the proceeds to all, as any had need. Every day they devoted themselves to meeting together in the temple,

and broke bread from house to house.
They ate their food with joyful and sincere hearts, praising God and enjoying the
favor of all the people. Every day the Lord
added to their number those who were
being saved. (Acts 2:42–47)

You can see in this passage from Acts that the early
church devoted themselves to God and each other
through both corporate gatherings (the temple) and in
the home (house to house). You can also see an outline for
what every small group should strive to achieve.

Discipleship

The text says, "They devoted themselves to the apostles' teaching." In other words, they were learning what
it means to be more like Christ through the apostles.
Creating disciples who then create disciples should
always be the final goal of any small group. Jesus made
this clear with His commission to His followers before
He returned to heaven:

"Go, therefore, and make disciples of
all nations, baptizing them in the name
of the Father and of the Son and of the
Holy Spirit, teaching them to observe
everything I have commanded you. And

remember, I am with you always, to the end of the age." (Matt. 28:19–20)

Therefore, we must always gather as a group, not just for the sake of gathering, but for the goal of helping people develop into mature believers. Note that Jesus did not say, "teaching them everything I have commanded you." He said, "teaching them to *observe* everything I have commanded you." Of course, we cannot observe what Jesus commanded unless we know what He commanded, but it needs to be clear that, though the study is important, the fruit of the study is what leads to fully devoted followers of Christ.

> We must always gather as a group, not just for the sake of gathering, but for the goal of helping people develop into mature believers.

Discipleship is not a static process. It will always involve movement toward something. If you want to know if people in your group are developing in their faith, look for these two movements in their lives.

Movement toward Christ

The original disciples followed in the footsteps of Jesus. Where He was leading, they were following. Consequently, their lives were becoming more like Christ as they followed closer and closer. The disciples in your group will begin to display more of the characteristics of Jesus as they move closer to Him.

Movement toward Others

Someone who is being discipled will want to share what they are experiencing with others. When Jesus changed the Samaritan woman's life with a conversation at the well, she ran immediately to tell everyone she knew to "Come, see a man who told me everything I ever did. Could this be the Messiah?" (John 4:29). When your life has been changed by the gospel, you want to tell everyone.

Community

The early church members "ate their food with joyful and sincere hearts, praising God and enjoying the favor of all the people" (Acts 2:46–47). Discipleship is a team sport. I have never enjoyed a meal as much when I am dining alone as when I am eating with a group of friends. Every small group meeting should include elements of building community and having fun. God did not create us to live in isolation.

You can see it modeled with the perfect relationship of the Trinity in Genesis:

> Then God said, "Let Us make man in Our image, according to Our likeness. They

> will rule the fish of the sea, the birds of the
> sky, the livestock, all the earth, and the
> creatures that crawl on the earth." (Gen.
> 1:26 HCSB)

And then prayed for by Jesus with His final prayer before His death on the cross:

> "May they all be one, as You, Father, are in
> Me and I am in You. May they also be one
> in Us, so the world may believe You sent
> Me." (John 17:21 HCSB)

Just as the Father, Son, and Holy Spirit have existed from all eternity in perfect community, God has created us in His image in order to live in biblical community. Our unity displays the oneness of God in the Trinity.

Mission

It's important that what we gain through being discipled in community is not just left there. Jesus expects us to be out making a difference in every environment we find ourselves. He said:

> "You are the light of the world. A city
> situated on a hill cannot be hidden. No one
> lights a lamp and puts it under a basket,
> but rather on a lampstand, and it gives
> light for all who are in the house. In the

same way, let your light shine before others, so that they may see your good works
and give glory to your Father in heaven."
(Matt. 5:14–16)

Your small group should always look for opportunities to serve missionally in the community around you.
Being on mission is not just a quarterly event, but a
lifestyle attained by group members. We will hit more
specifics on how you do this in a later chapter, but our
mandate as a fellowship of believers is to reach out
beyond our walls to the people who need what we have.
This is the essence of the gospel. Our small group is the
intersection of the gospel and real life. The good news of
what Jesus Christ did for us needs to go beyond our group
into the world.

Balance Is Important

While your group should have all three of those
biblical life elements running through it—discipleship,
community, and mission—there will be seasons where
it is out of balance. The initial spiritual makeup of the
group will help dictate where the group spends most of
its energy in the beginning.

Community will be the easiest to achieve and where
groups will gravitate to. It's important to make sure community is taking place from the beginning of the group,

but you will need to navigate the group toward discipleship and mission as group members get more comfortable with each other.

If your group is made up of mostly mature Christians, then there will also be times when a Bible study may seem more important than reaching those outside the group who need Christ. When that is clear, remind the group about the commission to reach the world with the gospel. There may be times where a study needs to be interrupted to give energy to serving outside the group.

The One-Anothers

Another beautiful example from the early church is how often they ministered to one another. The transliterated Greek word for the term "each other" is *allelon*, and it's used fifty-eight times in the New Testament. Here are just a few uses of the term:

- Meet together and encourage one another (Heb. 10:25)
- Encourage each other (1 Thess. 4:18)
- Love each other like brothers and sisters (Rom. 12:10)
- By helping each other with your troubles, you truly obey the law of Christ (Gal. 6:2)

- Care the same for each other (1 Cor. 12:25)
- Pray for each other (James 5:16)
- Serve each other with love (Gal. 5:13)
- Forgive each other (Col. 3:13)

It becomes clear as you read through the Bible that we were not meant to walk through life on our own. The original small group spent a majority of their time taking care of one another's needs.

By practicing the one-anothers, they also allowed members to discover and use their spiritual gifts within the group. You can see examples of the gifts—apostleship, discernment, encouragement, evangelism, faith, giving, healing, helps, hospitality, intercession, leadership, administration, mercy, miracles, prophecy, pastoring, teaching, wisdom, and knowledge—woven through the acts of service toward each other.

Creating biblical community in a small group is allowing room for the Holy Spirit to minister to and through group members. As each person is growing spiritually, they will discover their spiritual gifts and, in turn disciple someone else. This is how generations of disciples are created and leaders are developed.

My Experience

Our groups have taken various forms over the years. They all look different. Don't be afraid to change things up and try different approaches to what biblical community can look like. For instance, a few of our groups started to become too social and we discovered that not everyone was growing spiritually. When that was recognized, we took a step back to start asking questions to determine where everyone was on their spiritual journey. We found that one group member had never prayed in public, one was afraid to lead because of a past imprisonment, and another needed ideas on how to build a daily devotional time. It's okay to course-correct occasionally to help the group find its spiritual balance again.

QUESTIONS TO THINK ABOUT

1. What stood out to you the most in this chapter?

_____

_____

2. Do you believe the community the early church found can be replicated today? Why or why not?

_____

_____

3. What does it mean to you to disciple someone?

_____

_____

4. Who is someone you can begin to personally disciple today?

_____

_____

5. Which element of biblical life will be the most difficult for your group to achieve: discipleship, community, or mission?

_____

_____

6. Do you have any ideas for reaching outside of your group to help others?

_____

_____

CHAPTER 3

Preparing for Your Small Group

N ow that you have taken the faith leap of leading a small group, you want to make sure that your group is set up for success and ready to launch. As much as we would love for community to happen organically, a good system will give a framework for that community to grow.

Try to imagine the details for the group as a trellis in a garden. A trellis is a structure you put in your garden to help plants grow in the direction they are supposed to. Otherwise, the vines from the plants may grow "organically," but they will go everywhere and eventually choke out the other plants. When there is a trellis, the plants will wrap around the framework of the structure to grow straight up and healthy.

Well-planned details will be the trellis for the small group. They will help shape the direction and culture of the group. A poorly planned small group will eventually choke out the life of the group.

Answering the following four questions will help you go through those key details before the group launches.

Where Will the Group Be Located?

You have many choices of where the weekly group meeting will take place, and each choice has pros and cons.

A Home

A natural location for your small group to meet is in your home, or the home of other group members who are willing to consistently host. Hosting a group in a home helps create community faster than most other locations, but there are a few things to think about before you decide on this option:

- How many people can the home comfortably fit? The discussion time will need a room where everyone has a chair and can easily see each other. This will help foster an atmosphere of conversation and not teaching—think circles, not rows. You will also need to plan for a place for children if childcare will be offered.

- Is your home located in a geographically centered location for potential group members? For community to happen outside the group time, most group members will need to be less than a twenty-minute drive from the meeting location. There may be special circumstances for a few types of groups, but for most groups to thrive, the meeting location needs to be centrally located.

- Will you be available to host a small group for several consecutive weeks? Meeting weekly is the best rhythm for a group to bond quickly. Groups that only meet once a month will never gain the relational equity it takes to build loyalty. Even groups who meet every other week will struggle with consistency. If a member misses one or two meetings in a row, they will likely disconnect from the life of the group and drop out. Groups who meet every week have a much higher rate of success.

A Neighborhood Clubhouse

Many neighborhoods have nice clubhouses that sit empty most nights of the week. They sometimes come with a nominal cleaning fee but are often free to people living in the neighborhood or apartment complex. They are not as instantly comfortable as someone's home, but they do offer a large gathering space for the group discussion time. Childcare can be an issue at a clubhouse with only one large room.

A Room at the Church Building

Your church may offer nights during the week where groups can use classrooms as a meeting location. The obvious benefit is having a central location where most group members already go every week. Also, depending on the policies of the church, there will be available rooms where childcare can take place. The downside of meeting at the church is the lack of intimacy offered in a classroom as opposed to someone's home. Offering food can also be more difficult if there's not an available kitchen.

A Break Room at the Office

Many offices will allow a Bible study to take place onsite as long as it's voluntary and done during official break times. If you choose this option, it will limit who you can invite but will offer you the opportunity to disciple people outside your normal neighborhood and family circles. The choice of study is more critical in this setting. You will need a study that fits the time and space constraints of an office setting. A video-enhanced study would be difficult to facilitate, but a book study would work well in a break room.

A Third Space

Some groups choose "third spaces" like coffee shops or restaurants to meet. There are a few benefits to these locations for smaller groups of five or less. For example, it could provide a good place to meet early in the morning without having to host and could give group members the chance to build relationships with servers and other regulars, with whom they can share the gospel. However, with mid-size or larger groups, seating and distraction become huge obstacles. If your group is more than five, I recommend avoiding third spaces unless you have no other viable options.

What Day and Time Will the Group Meet?

The next decision you will need to make is what day of the week and time of day the group will meet. This decision is not inconsequential because what you choose will filter out or in who can be a part of the group.

If you choose a night during the week, parents with young children may have a difficult time due to early bedtimes and school activities. Choosing Saturday may interfere with weekend ball games. If you live in the South, Friday night high school football is a big deal and difficult to compete with. (I know this one from experience.)

A later start time will work well for young professionals used to staying out later but may eliminate people with early alarm clocks. One of our first small groups had a morning radio host who had to be at her job at 4:00 a.m. I didn't blame her for nodding off a few times during the group discussion.

I find that Sunday afternoons typically work well for parents with young children, and weeknights with later start times are great for young professionals just getting off work. The day and time will also affect what you offer for food—and you should offer something. You can just have snacks and drinks with a later weeknight time, but should offer dinner if your start time means people are coming straight from work to group.

When Should We Launch the Group?

Once you decide the day and time for the group, you will need to pick a date to launch. There are times of the year that work best for group launches and will help ensure that your small group gets off to a strong start.

You will want to choose a launch date that will allow your group to meet for several weeks before an interruption.

A January or February start date is a great time to kick off a new or relaunched small group. People often make New Year's resolutions to go to church and get connected in community, and you can take advantage of that momentum by kicking your group off in mid-to-late January or early February. However, you will want to avoid starting the group on Super Bowl Sunday, unless you are starting with friends who would like to watch the game together at your house.

Another good opportunity to launch your group is after school starts in August or early September. People are back from vacations and holidays and getting back into a weekly schedule during those months. You can also take advantage of inviting unconnected people who may have moved into your community during the summer. You will want to avoid launching your group on Labor Day weekend unless it's with a group of friends who will naturally get together for the holiday.

If Easter falls early enough on the calendar, post-Easter is also a good time to launch a group off of the crowds of Easter Sunday. If you choose this time to launch, make sure you have at least six weeks before the unofficial beginning of summer: Memorial Day weekend. That will allow your group to go through a full Bible study and gel before the craziness of summer vacations starts.

Summer and the holiday season of Thanksgiving/ Christmas are not ideal times to launch a small group.

The group will not have enough time to bond before being interrupted by vacations and events.

How Long Should the Group Meet?

Depending on the time of year you start your group, the initial run of the group will be determined by the calendar. If you kick off your group at the beginning of the year, choose a study that will take you up to Easter. The Easter week can then serve as a short break before starting your next study that will end before Memorial Day.

A post-Easter start date will call for a four- to six-week study before you're forced to break your weekly meeting rhythm for summer.

If you are starting your group in August or September, look for a study or two that can take your group to the Thanksgiving holiday. If your group is planning to continue to meet through the school year to the summer break, you have the option to choose a longer study, like through an entire book of the Bible, with short breaks around the holidays.

Planning Matters

Preparing well for your small group may seem overwhelming and peripheral to the heart of the group, but poor planning will derail the mission of creating disciples. Your members may not point out when meetings go smoothly but will likely not return if there is too much disorganization. Taking time at the beginning to think through every detail will help leave room for the Holy Spirit to do His work during your times together.

My Experience

We love to eat at our small groups, but after five years of planning meals and organizing who was bringing what dish, my wife was tired. We decided with the launch of a new young professionals group to have a later start time and just have people bring snacks. Not every type of group needs a five-course meal to be successful.

QUESTIONS TO THINK ABOUT

1. What stood out to you the most in this chapter?

_____

_____

2. Does putting together details excite you or paralyze you? Is there someone in your group who loves details that can help you prepare?

_____

_____

3. What is the best location for your group to meet? What are the positives and negatives to choosing that location?

_____

_____

4. What type of group member are you hoping to attract? What day and time will make the group most accessible for them?

_____

_____

5. What is the best launch date for your small group?

_____

_____

CHAPTER 4

Group Type Trade-Offs

There are a few decisions for your group that will have trade-offs depending on the decision you make. You will need to decide what direction will be best for the long-term health of your particular small group.

Open vs. Closed

An important decision to make is whether to be an open group or a closed group. Open groups are simply open to new people joining through the life of the group, and closed groups may be open for the first week or two of the group but will then close to new people until the end of the life of the group.

Case for Open Groups

Groups that choose to stay open to new members have a missional mentality that welcomes people who need biblical community. Having your group stay open also helps multiply the effectiveness of the church reaching people quickly with the gospel. Church buildings only have so much room for groups to form community, but there is no limit when we take our community outside those walls.

We sometimes picture small groups as a way to get current church attenders into biblical community, but think about how much more effective an invitation to your church would be if it came through an invitation to be a part of your small group first.

- They will have already been exposed to the pastor's teachings if you are doing a sermon-based study.
- There is a built-in follow-up through the group meetings.
- There is no rush to get them there on a Sunday.
- The invite starts and continues with a relationship.

If groups are to become the new front door of the church, they have to start with our neighborhoods. Our world has changed so that most people don't know their neighbors anymore. When I was growing up, our neighbors were a natural extension of our family. We knew all of our immediate neighbors, and I spent almost as much time in their houses as I did in mine. The thought of inviting a neighbor to your church wasn't that scary at all.

Now, you are lucky to get a cursory wave before the garage door goes down and your neighbors disappear into the house. Who has time for connecting with neighbors anymore? When we first moved to Nashville, most of the houses in our neighborhood had garage entrances on the back of the house. The only way to catch your neighbor was by chasing their car down the driveway and performing a drop-and-roll maneuver under their garage door before it could shut! I couldn't understand why my neighbor wouldn't talk to me again after I did this the first time . . .

> Groups that choose to stay open to new members have a missional mentality that welcomes people who need biblical community.

Here are a few ideas to connect with your neighbors who are not already plugged into the church or a small group:

- Throw a block party. Opportunities begin as relationships, and block parties set the stage for future friendships.

- Host a movie on your lawn for the families in the neighborhood. Put out a few flyers around the neighborhood and fire up the latest Pixar hit.
- Take part in neighborhood-sponsored events like Easter egg hunts or quarterly "spruce up the neighborhood" days.
- Organize welcome baskets for new people in the neighborhood. You can also include an invitation flyer to your group in the basket.

Case for Closed Groups

Some groups will choose to stay closed for the life of the group, or until the group members decide to open for new people. We can see this type of group modeled for us with Jesus' small group. Once He had chosen His twelve, the group was not open to new members until Judas was replaced after the betrayal in the garden.

There are several benefits to staying closed as a group:

- Accountability can be stronger when the group is full of people who know each other well and are comfortable being vulnerable with one another.

Inviting someone new into that group can disrupt the needed intimacy.

- It takes at least three months of consistently meeting together before most of the relational walls come down. We call those "refrigerator rights" in our group. When a group member feels comfortable enough to walk into our house and open the refrigerator without asking permission first, that's when you know you have bonded as a family. Inviting a new person or couple into the group will reset the time to get to the refrigerator rights.

- A few groups, like recovery groups, will by necessity need to remain closed for the life of the group. A more discipleship-intensive group of three or four people meeting outside group time will need to be closed as well.

The choice of being an open or closed group should be determined before the first meeting and included in the group covenant. (We'll return to this concept later.) The group members need to know if they are encouraged to invite guests, or if the group will close for community and accountability reasons.

Short-Term vs. Ongoing

A short-term group is designed to only last a few weeks before either disbanding, multiplying, or continuing on with new members. An ongoing group will stay together for at least eighteen to twenty-four months before disbanding, multiplying, or continuing on with new members. There are benefits to both approaches.

Case for Short-Term

A short-term group can be a gateway to small groups for people reticent about giving group life a try. A church may launch a few short-term groups for six to eight weeks to give the church body a taste of community outside a Sunday morning experience. Those groups may start on the church campus for six weeks with the goal of moving to homes after that initial period. One of our first small group experiences was a short-term group that met in the auditorium with other groups for eight weeks before we moved off into a home.

Short-term groups can also meet an immediate felt need around a specific topic for six to eight weeks. Those groups may focus on topics like finances, parenting skills, premarital issues, and spiritual growth. The goal for most short-term groups is to help people eventually be in an ongoing group.

Case for Ongoing

While short-term groups can be a bridge for people new to groups, the goal should be to land in an ongoing, long-term group with other believers. An eighteen- to twenty-four-month group gives enough time for a group to come together and help each other grow relationally and spiritually. As pointed out earlier in this chapter, it takes time to be comfortable with new people, and ongoing groups give you that time.

The potential downside to an ongoing group is the chance that it can, over time, become stale and unhealthy. A group that is ongoing and closed to new people will begin to have the same conversations around the same topics after two years. Changing the type of studies you are doing can help keep fresh perspectives. Also, opening the group up to new people can bring new thoughts to the conversations. An ongoing group should also look at multiplying after eighteen to twenty-four months, which we will explore in a later chapter.

> It takes time to be comfortable with new people, and ongoing groups give you that time.

On-Campus vs. Off-Campus

We briefly covered potential locations in chapter 3, but if your church traditionally only offers groups that meet on the church campus during a Sunday service, some thought must go into the trade-offs between hosting a group at the church on Sunday or off of the church campus during the week.

Case for On-Campus

- Groups are easier to join. The idea of showing up at someone's home for a group experience is daunting for many people—especially if they are new to the church and don't have a preestablished relationship with the small group leaders. It's much easier to step out of a church service and into a classroom for group time.
- There is built-in childcare. One of the main barriers for families joining groups is the childcare issue. It's also a barrier for potential group leaders. Not every home has adequate childcare space, and not every church can offer its groups great resources for childcare off-campus. You erase that barrier by providing groups that meet

on-campus during a church service with childcare available.

- There can be more consistency with the group. Staff members or group coaches can drop into a group on any weekend to help guide a new leader. Start and stop times are also better defined. A group leader doesn't have to worry about people sticking around for an hour or two after the group has officially ended.
- There is easier ongoing training for leaders. All the leaders are in one place every Sunday, so providing information and training can be accomplished by coming in thirty minutes early, or staying thirty minutes after. It is much more difficult to find a convenient time for off-campus leaders to gather in one location.

Case for Off-Campus

- It is easier to multiply groups. There are only so many rooms in a church building, and the trend is not to build more for educational space. Once those rooms are full at optimal times, there's nowhere else to go. Small

groups that meet off-campus can be
anywhere: homes, apartments, break
rooms, clubhouses . . . there is no limit
to where off-campus groups can go.

• There can be more transparency.
Because off-campus groups are not
restrained by hard time limits, there
is more time for members to share
their lives with each other. If a deeper
conversation is needed after the official group time ends, it can continue
in the kitchen. There's no pressure
from the third-grade class needing the
room for the next hour.

• Your group can have a greater missional
focus. The chances of a non-church
attender coming to an on-campus
group are low. Group members can
invite an unchurched neighbor to their
home for dinner with the small group.
Also, an invitation that starts with a
personal relationship is more likely to
result in a member sticking with the
group.

• Relationships have the opportunity to
go deeper. Sitting in your living room
invites conversations that would not
necessarily take place in a classroom.

Group members can get to know the leaders better by asking about pictures and mementos in the home. Kids are also a part of the life of the group by just being present in the house during the meeting.

With all of these trade-offs, you can see there is not one model that fits perfectly for every small group. My groups have found the most success being ongoing, open to new members, and meeting in a home, but that description may not fit who you are as a leader, the circumstances for your group, or the vision of your church. Weigh the pros and cons of each model to decide the best approach for your group.

My Experience

One of our groups used three different homes for the location. Each week was hosted in a different one. The upside to using a home rotation was the lesser burden on the hosts. They only had to prepare and clean for the group meeting once a month. The downside was the difficulty of getting consistency with a different location every week. It was also confusing if the schedule had to change at the last minute. We ultimately went back to one location for simplicity.

QUESTIONS TO THINK ABOUT

1. What stood out to you the most in this chapter?

_____

_____

2. Do you feel like your group should be open or closed? What are the benefits to both sides for your group?

_____

_____

3. Will your group start as a short-term or ongoing group?

_____

_____

4. If your group will start as a short-term group, how will you eventually transition to being ongoing?

_____

_____

5. If your group will start as an ongoing group, what steps will you take to keep it healthy?

_____

_____

Launching Your Small Group

CHAPTER 5

Recruiting and Advertising

N ow that you have thought through most of the logistical details of the group, it's time to decide who you will invite to the first meeting. The people on your invitation list will eventually be people you do life with. A majority of our closest friends in life have come through our small groups. They have become accountability partners, shoulders to cry on, people to laugh with, and ultimately, family.

That is why it is critical that you put a lot of thought into this list. You should also keep in mind that not everyone you invite will end up in the group, and not everyone who comes to the first or second meeting will stick with the group until the end. And that's okay. The people God sends to your group will be there for a reason and for a season.

The first thing you want to do is something we often do last: pray for the right people for your group. Pray that God will give you wisdom about whom to invite. Pray for those relationships to develop. And pray that the people you invite have open hearts and minds. By starting with prayer, you acknowledge that the formation of this small group is in God's hands.

After you have given it to God, sit down and make a list of potential people to invite. Start with the people in your inner circle. That list would include family members, neighbors, and coworkers—the people you may already do aspects of life with. After you have that initial list, broaden it to people just outside your inner circle—maybe someone you talk with at church who doesn't seem to be connected to a small group, or someone you're friendly with at work. There may also be a neighbor you wave at as you pass who could be open to an invitation. Most people are longing for deeper community, but don't know where to start. The invitation to your group may be that first step needed.

> The people God sends to your group will be there for a reason and for a season.

The Questions

Once you have a good-sized list, you will need to think through answers to inevitable questions that will come after the invite.

How much time is this going to take? People already have busy lives with church, work, and family commitments. They will need to know up front how much time committing to this group will add to that full plate. I recommend keeping the group meeting time to two hours or fewer. That time frame will help keep it reasonable to most people.

What are we going to do with our children during group meetings? This is the number-one question from parents, and the number-one barrier to many people committing to a small group. If you are planning to invite married couples with young kids, have a solution for this issue before the group begins. Here are a few ideas I recommend to group leaders:

- Each family makes their own arrangements for childcare.
- The group hires a babysitter, and the families split the cost. If another family lives in the same neighborhood, the children could be at one while the adults meet in the other. One of our small groups used this arrangement for a group season. Note that if

this is an official small group offered through the church, be sure to check with church leadership on official policies for vetting babysitters. You may need to obtain background checks on potential childcare workers.

- Work with the student ministry to hire a female babysitter who is raising money for a summer missions trip.
- Work out a co-op relationship with another group that meets on another night.
- Make one night a month a game night where the kids are invited to take part.
- Involve the older kids into the discussion and life of the group. My kids have been active members of our groups through the years.
- Rotate childcare among the members of the group, putting two non-related adults in charge of babysitting for a given night, and rotating each week.

Will there be homework? This question also speaks to the busyness issue. Potential group members will need to know what extra time this commitment will add on top of the weekly group meeting time. I recommend choosing a study that requires little-to-no homework. Book studies are difficult for most people to handle because of the reading time involved. A well-designed study will eliminate the need for homework, but offer extra Bible study and questions if desired.

Am I going to have to talk during meetings? Extroverts will have no problem jumping right into the discussion, but introverts like me may take a little longer to feel comfortable enough to open up to the group. Be ready to reassure people that you will not force them to talk until they are comfortable. Good, open-ended icebreaker questions at the beginning of the discussion time can help everyone feel more at ease with sharing.

Will I have to pray out loud? This is a big deal for many people, especially if you are planning on inviting seekers or new Christians. I will never call on someone to pray aloud in the group unless I am sure they are ready for it.

Who else will be in the group? Be ready to share the demographics of the group in the invitation or advertisement. Most people want to be in community with other people in the same life-stage. If this group is specifically for young married couples, make that clear from the beginning.

How much do I have to know about the Bible? The people you will invite are in different stages on their spiritual journey. Keeping that in mind, the study you choose should be conversational and not filled with a lot of insider Christian language. You want something that

challenges mature believers but is accessible to baby
Christians.

How many weeks or months is the group going to last?
Be up front with the expectation for the longevity of the
commitment. Most people will not be ready to jump into
a long-term commitment yet. A six- to twelve-week run
with a short break before the next study will give them
the peace of mind to try the group waters first before
committing long term.

*If I don't like it, can I leave without people being angry
with me?* It's a good idea to start the first week with
something informal—like a dinner at a restaurant—to
give potential group members the opportunity to test the
group out before the study begins.

What are we going to do during meetings? I was very
unsure of what a small group did before I joined one. I
imagined all kinds of weird things, from confessing your
gravest sin during the first meeting, to everyone group
hugging at the end. Give potential group members a clear
picture of what will take place each week in your invitation. (And try your best not to make it too weird!)

Make the Ask

After you have made a list of potential invitees and
come up with answers to the inevitable questions, it's
time to make the ask. If the idea of being in a small group
is completely foreign to someone, it will take a little bit of

time and convincing before they are sitting in your living room.

An in-person invitation is always best. Give the person a call or shoot them an email to ask if you can talk for a few minutes at church or over coffee. During your meeting, start with the "why" for your small group. It will go something like this: "We are starting this small group for young married couples who want to go deeper in God's Word and learn how to navigate life together. We have prayed about who should be in the group, and we feel you and your husband would be a great addition." Follow this invitation up with the logistics of the group and answer any questions they might have.

Don't expect or even ask for a commitment on the spot. If they decide to commit, that's great! But most people will need time to think and pray about it before deciding. They may also need to check in with their spouse before giving an answer. Let them know you will check back in a week, either in person or by a phone call. If they decide that this is not the best time to be in a small group, that's okay. Tell them you will keep them in mind for future opportunities to join the group. I have invited people several times to my groups before they joined. The right season of life or circumstance will come along for them to need the community you are offering through your group. Don't give up!

Advertising Your Group

If you cannot fill your group through personal invites, it's a good idea to advertise the group through your church or neighborhood.

Many churches will offer group launches where small groups list their group in the church bulletin, in a newsletter, or online at the church website. If you advertise this way, you will want to have a clear and compelling description for the group. The potential group members need to know what they are signing up for in two to three sentences.

You may also meet potential group members by being a part of a small groups fair or connect event at the church. This will give you the opportunity to meet them in person and pitch them the benefits of your group in a few minutes. If you take part in a groups fair, work on a three- to five-minute version of why your group exists and why they might want to be in it.

You can also advertise the group through your neighborhood by putting together a professional-looking flyer with the group details and distributing them to your neighbors. Some neighborhoods and apartment complexes also have a community board you can hang flyers on. If you advertise this way, be sure to have a good way for them to contact you and be prompt about responding.

Social media can also be an effective way to advertise your group. You can put it on your personal Facebook page or any local Facebook Groups you belong to. Clear it with group administrators before you add it to their group's page.

After you have made invitations and advertised your group, rest knowing that God will send the people that need this community. Continue to pray for His guidance as you move into the next stage of leading your newly formed small group.

My Experience

Our most consistent group members have normally come from individual invites. However, we have also had success from advertising our group through the church. Our current small group began that way. We decided this time to open our group up to anyone, at any stage of life, who lives in our area. It has been fun to see the different perspectives that come from people not in the same stage of life as us. We would have never had some of these conversations if we had limited it to only people in our personal circles and similar life stages.

QUESTIONS TO THINK ABOUT

1. What stood out to you the most in this chapter?

_____

_____

2. What is your biggest fear in inviting people to your group?

_____

_____

3. Who do you need to invite first to the group?

_____

_____

4. Which potential question will be the most difficult to answer?

_____

_____

5. Where are the most effective places for you to advertise your group?

_____

_____

6. What is your three- to five-sentence purpose statement for your group?

_____

_____

CHAPTER 6

Kicking the Group Off Right

Making a good first impression is critical for the ultimate success of the small group. You only get one chance at a first impression, so thinking through all the details around that kickoff is critical.

The initial location does not have to be in the location where the group will regularly meet. You may choose to have that first meeting at a neutral location like a restaurant or a room at the church. A neutral location can sometimes help people ease into the life of the group. Meeting people at a restaurant is less intimidating than showing up at a stranger's home the first time. If you decide on a restaurant, choose one that is affordable and has enough room for the whole group to gather around one or two tables.

Good and thorough communication before that first meeting is important. The group members will need an email stating the location and time the group will start. Don't assume everyone will read through the first email; a follow-up email the day of the meeting is also necessary as a reminder. Include your phone number for anyone who gets lost or has last-minute questions. If your first meeting is in a home, arrange the chairs in a circle so everyone faces each other. This will help promote conversation and not the expectation that someone will teach the study. If you are using a video-enhanced study, arrange the room for everyone to comfortably see the television or screen.

Provide name tags for everyone for the first several meetings and whenever someone new visits the group. Having name tags will help the group build community faster. It will also help newcomers not feel as awkward during their first visit. I always have trouble remembering names, so my groups will wear name tags for the first six weeks of meetings.

The Group Covenant

It's always a good idea to begin with a group covenant or agreement. This document will state the facts and values the group will abide by for the duration of the group's life (example in the Resources Appendix). Starting with a covenant helps set expectations for group participation.

A good covenant can cover most of the issues that might arise in your group. Group members can also add to the covenant as the group finds its identity. A few details to include on the covenant are location and starting time of the group each week, childcare arrangements, and food expectations.

With a group covenant, members are committing to:

- grow healthy spiritual lives by building a healthy community
- give priority to the group meeting and to call as soon as possible if they will be absent or late
- create a safe place where people can be heard, feel loved (no quick answers, snapping to judgment, or simple fixes), and know that anything that is shared is confidential and will not be discussed outside the group
- give the group permission to speak into their lives and help them to live a healthy, balanced spiritual life that is pleasing to God
- build relationships by getting to know each other and praying for each other regularly
- invite their friends who might benefit from the group

- recognize the importance of helping others experience community by
  eventually multiplying and starting a
  new group

Staying on Time

It's important that you strive to begin and end the group at the times agreed upon in the group covenant. Members will consistently show up late if the starting time does not seem important to the leader, and people with childcare commitments will struggle if the meeting goes too long. Although there will be occasional exceptions, there are a few things you can do to help keep the meeting on schedule.

Share the food responsibilities with the group. Group members responsible for bringing food are more likely to be on time or early. They understand the group will be waiting on them if they are late.

Don't wait on everyone to arrive before starting. If your group has agreed to a 6:00 p.m. start time, commit to start promptly with the people who are there.

Keep the first twenty minutes informal. The first part of the meeting should be reserved for just hanging out and eating together. Providing this open time is crucial, especially if the group is new and still getting to know each other.

Have a time schedule in mind for the meeting. Calculate ahead of the meeting how much time each element should take and try to stick to it. Keep in mind that if the study includes a video teaching portion, it will cut into some allotted discussion time. However, don't be so rigid that there isn't room for the Holy Spirit to work in the meeting. There will be moments where the group needs to stay on a question or a discussion point for more clarity. Be prepared to make adjustments as you go.

Have a transition in mind to get the group to the finish line of the discussion. You always want the discussion to end with action points for the group to carry out immediately. Keep this finish line in mind during the conversation and be ready to transition to it with enough time left for prayer.

Aim to end the meeting fifteen minutes early. Ending a little early will give enough time at the end for group members to continue the conversation informally before heading home. Some of the best discussions will occur after the official study time has concluded. This will be especially true for members who did not feel comfortable speaking up in front of the group. Leave room for those catalytic one-on-one conversations over dessert.

Be available after group, but keep some boundaries. There will be occasions where a group member may need to stay after for an extended conversation or prayer. You should be available, but be aware if it's a habitual practice for someone. He may need to be gently reminded about boundaries you have in place for family time. You are in this for the long haul; personal and family health should always be guarded.

Between the Meetings

Most life-change opportunities will occur outside the normal meeting times, so it's important for the group to stay connected throughout the week. You can utilize technology and "old school" methods to help group members connect outside meetings.

Group roster. Provide emails, phone numbers, and social media handles to everyone (roster example in the Resources Appendix) at the first meeting. You can also use apps like GroupMe to keep everyone up on the latest news and schedule for the group. Group members can easily opt out of push notifications if the app gets too busy.

> Most life-change opportunities will occur outside the normal meeting times, so it's important for the group to stay connected throughout the week.

Email prayer lists. Prayer list emails will help keep needs in front of group members during the week. Also, plan on following up on requests during the group prayer time. A good leader is a praying leader. Spend time each week praying for each group member.

Private Facebook pages. Facebook is great for keeping the conversation going between meetings. You can also plan social events and missional opportunities on your page. The Facebook Live feature can be used for live discussions or training in between meetings. Another idea is to use your Facebook page to facilitate a discussion around an online Bible study during busy months, like summer, when the group is not meeting every week for a study. Smallgroup.com has thousands of studies to choose from that can be facilitated virtually.

Group texting apps. Apps are helpful for sending urgent needs and last-minute updates. Just be careful to not overuse this tool. Your group members will tire of over-texting and will opt out.

Handwritten notes. In our world of the digital and the immediate, an old-fashioned handwritten note can go a long way. If someone in the group comes to mind during your prayer time, drop them a quick note to say you are thinking about and praying for them.

Offline coffee meetings. Choose a group member of the same sex to invite to coffee outside group time. You will learn a lot more about that person in that informal setting than you will ever discover during a group meeting. Don't put an agenda on it, just commit to learning more of their story.

Church services. Commit as a group to sit together during the weekend services. This will occasionally carry over to lunch or brunch after services for more informal bonding time.

Kids' activities. If a group member's child has a soccer game, go to the game and cheer loudly! We have had members of our groups come to almost all of our kids' major activities. Loving on my kids will bond us for life.

If No One Shows Up . . .

It can be very disheartening to prepare for your group and then have no one show up. It's sometimes worse if only one person comes! Here are a few factors to think about if no one signs up or shows up for the group:

- Is the group being hosted in too remote of an area from the church? It will be more difficult to ask church members to attend a group that is over fifteen to twenty minutes from their house. If this is the case, you will need to work harder at building your group from your immediate social and neighborhood circles.

- Is the group's focus too narrow? Targeting a specific cause for a group to form around can be beneficial, but it will take longer to gain traction. A specific support-type group will need more time before critical mass in the group is achieved.

- Are you meeting on an unpopular night? Trying to host a group on Friday nights in a community where high school football shuts the town down every week will probably be a tough go.
- Are the meetings consistent enough? Groups that only meet once a month will never gain the relational equity it takes to build loyalty. Even groups that meet every other week will struggle with consistency. If a member misses one or two meetings in a row, they will get disconnected from the life of the group and will drop out. Groups that meet every week have a much higher rate of success. Avoid cancelling a meeting if only a few members cannot make it.
- Is the group shrinking? It is always good to add new people during the life of the small group. Groups will inevitably shrink if new people aren't being added. Eventually, you will end up with a good solid core that attends weekly.

My Experience

Not every group my wife and I have led has been a great success. When we moved to a new city a few years ago, we purposefully picked our new home based on how easy it would be to host a large number of people. The kitchen was spacious for pre-discussion time, and the living room had plenty of room to arrange chairs around the outside. We had as many as forty-four people crammed into our house one time. Our first couple of groups in that home averaged ten to fifteen couples, so we felt confident that the system was working and we knew what would attract people to our group. That was true—right up until we opened the sign-up sheet for the third semester and only one couple committed to our group. Even though we continued to invite (or beg) other people to join, our small group stayed truly small the entire semester. It was never a difficult decision to cancel a group meeting; when the other couple couldn't make it, it was cancelled. Not every group you start will take off immediately.

QUESTIONS TO THINK ABOUT

1. What stood out to you the most in this chapter?

_____

_____

2. What type of location would be best for the first group meeting?

_____

_____

3. What details need to be included in your initial communication to the group?

_____

_____

4. What guidelines need to be in the group covenant?

_____

_____

5. How can you use social media to help the group connect outside the group time?

_____

_____

6. Are there any factors that would keep people from coming to the group? If there are, how can you eliminate them?

_____

_____

Leading Your
Small Group

CHAPTER 7

Facilitating a
Group Meeting

Acore component of leading a small group meeting will be facilitating the conversation through the Bible study. Even though you may not be teaching a lesson, there are still little things you can do and watch for that will help guide the group to a spiritually impactful discussion.

Asking Good Questions

The leader's main role during the discussion time is to ask questions. Asked in the right way, those questions will lead to a thought-provoking discussion that forces the group to dive deeper into the Scripture behind that week's focus.

If you study the ministry of Jesus, you notice He asked a lot of questions. Here are just a few:

- "Can any of you add one moment to his life span by worrying?" (Matt. 6:27)
- "Why do you look at the splinter in your brother's eye but don't notice the beam of wood in your own eye?" (Matt. 7:3)
- "Why are you afraid, you of little faith?" (Matt. 8:26)
- "You of little faith, why did you doubt?" (Matt. 14:31)
- "Who do people say that the Son of Man is?" (Matt. 16:13)
- "Why do you call me 'Lord, Lord,' and don't do the things I say?" (Luke 6:46)

Jesus asked questions because He wanted His listeners to go beyond hearing and start thinking. He knew the answers—He is God, after all—but people needed to learn to think for themselves. This style of teaching brought everyone into the narrative.

In the same way, we want our group members to bring themselves into the study by answering three types of questions: What? Now what? So what?

What?

What (does the Bible say?) questions force us to look at what the Scripture says first. A well-written topical study will give the facilitator multiple Scriptures for a complete perspective on a subject. Beware of studies based on just one Scripture or pieces of Scripture. We want our group to know what the whole Bible says to us. A more in-depth exegetical study of a book of the Bible should be accompanied by a Bible commentary for more perspective.

Now What?

Now what (should I believe?) questions cause us to examine what type of heart change we need to make considering the Scriptures we studied. All of us come to discussions with preexisting beliefs or suppositions. Our conclusions should always line up with the message of the cross. The gospel is the only way to heart change. Help your group wade through these "now what" questions with the truth of the gospel as the measuring stick.

So What?

So what (difference should that make in how I live?) questions lead to immediate application of what has been studied. The group members should never walk away from the discussion without clear points on how to live out the gospel in their daily lives. James 1:22 tells us to "be doers of the word and not hearers only." The ultimate success of the study is the action taken because of it.

Good questions should also be open-ended. If a question asks for a "yes" or "no" or some other one-word answer, rephrase the question or skip it. You can also follow it up with, "Why did you answer that way?"

Don't feel obligated to ask every question in the study. You may find that certain questions need more time for in-depth discussion, or some questions can be skipped to keep the meeting on track. There are no prizes for finishing every question.

Use an icebreaker question at the beginning of the discussion to help everyone feel more comfortable using their voices. A good icebreaker will be easy to answer and reveal something interesting about the person. Icebreaker questions should stay light and broad for the first few meetings and then focus more as the group is more established. There are examples of great icebreakers in the Resources Appendix of this book.

The Power of Silence

We are afraid of silence, especially as small group leaders. If there is silence in the room, that means no one is talking, and if no one is talking, then we are surely failing as facilitators. Right?

I believe we are missing out on an effective tool if we are so afraid of silence that we completely eliminate it from a group meeting. There is something powerful about creating intentional space in a group meeting. In fact, there are examples throughout the Bible where silence and solitude are commended:

- After the earthquake there was a fire, but the LORD was not in the fire. And after the fire there was a voice, a soft whisper. (1 Kings 19:12)
- A time to tear and a time to sew; a time to be silent and a time to speak. (Eccl. 3:7)
- My dear brothers and sisters, understand this: Everyone should be quick to listen, slow to speak, and slow to anger. (James 1:19)
- I am at rest in God alone; my salvation comes from Him. (Ps. 62:1 HCSB)

I believe we are missing out on an effective tool if we are so afraid of silence that we completely eliminate it from a group meeting.

So how do we plan for and best use the power of silence in our small groups? Here are three ways to take advantage of silence in your group:

Use Silence to Encourage Group Members to Speak

It seems like an oxymoron to use silence as a tool for participation, but it works. An effective facilitator should only talk 30 percent of the time. Remember that you have read the questions ahead of time. It will take everyone else a few moments to process the material before they are ready to answer. It's uncomfortable to let a question sit there for a few beats, but if you can let the awkwardness go, someone will break the silence. You can miss a great conversation by speaking too soon.

Use Silence to Allow a Moment to Sink In

There will be moments during a Bible study where the group needs a few seconds to take in what was just read or said. Effective speakers use pauses in their speeches to make important points resonate. The same principle applies to group discussions. The next time a powerful verse is read or someone makes a thought-provoking comment, pause a second or two before moving on. Those two seconds of silence will make the moment's impact last.

Use Silence to Meditate on Scripture

Before launching right into prayer time at the end of the discussion, take a few moments to allow the group to meditate on the Scripture from the Bible study. Ask someone to read a key verse or two aloud and then be silent as you allow God's Word to prepare your hearts for prayer. This time doesn't have to be long—maybe two to three minutes—but fight the temptation to break in too soon. Meditation can help lead to application.

The 4 D's

Almost every group will have one or more of what I call "EGRs." EGR stands for: Extra Grace Required. These are well-meaning but high-demanding people who can derail a group discussion if not dealt with in a healthy, biblical way.

The Dominator

Your group may have at least one member who has a tendency to dominate the conversation. They have been a Christian for a while, and it's difficult for them to let others express their thoughts first. Here are a few ideas you can try with a dominator:

- Sit next to him or her during the discussion time. There is something about that proximity to the facilitator that can help quiet a dominator.
- Don't make eye contact first with the person when you ask a question to the group.

- Intentionally ask another group member a question directly before offering it to the group.
- Meet with him or her after the group time to ask for help in giving less seasoned Christians in the group the opportunity to express their thoughts first.

The Dodger

Opposite of the dominator, the dodger is the person in the group who never enters the conversation. They never make eye contact and seem disengaged with group life. Here are a few things you can do to engage the dodgers in your group:

- Don't force someone to talk in the group before they are ready to. Some people just need time to feel comfortable with the group before they can open up.
- Give everyone in the group the opportunity to share their story in five minutes or fewer. You need to give them at least a week's notice before sharing.
- Ask for her opinion on a question that is not too intrusive or difficult. Icebreaker questions like, "What

superhero did you want to be growing up?" are ideal for getting everyone into the conversation and comfortable using their voices.

- Arrange for coffee or a chat outside the group time. Many people are more comfortable opening up one-on-one rather than in a large group.

The Debater

You will hit topics in your group that will be controversial to some. In fact, if you are committed to studying the whole Bible, that will definitely be the case. When that happens, you may have people in your group who want to debate either side of the issue. Some debate is healthy, and leaders must learn to differentiate between primary gospel issues and secondary issues. On primary issues—for example, the full humanity and divinity of Christ, the reality of Christ as the only way of salvation, and the necessity of sharing the gospel with the world—God's truth must ultimately be agreed upon. On less important matters—for example, debates about finer doctrinal points like the definition of predestination or views on the end times—it's okay to leave some disagreement. Ultimately, the goal of your group is discipleship, not mere theological training. Here are a few things you can do to keep that goal in sight:

- Know what God is telling us in the passage of Scripture being discussed. This will involve preparation.
- Study the passage in context with the group. This will shed more light on the issue than just a few verses.
- Refer to a study Bible like the *CSB Study Bible*. Study Bibles can help explain difficult passages.
- Never be afraid to end a debate with, "Let me check with a pastor this week and report back to the group on this question." It's okay to not know the answer in the moment.

The Drainer

A drainer is someone who always seems to drain the life out of the group. They are the constant Debbie Downer. No matter what the topic of discussion is that week, they turn it into a conversation about them and their current struggles. A drainer will make other group members hesitant to open up about their own personal lives. Here are a few things you can do to help manage the drainer in your group:

- Meet with the person outside the group time to bring the issue to their attention. They may not realize the problem and will be more aware of their comments in future meetings.

- If the prayer time is normally done through verbal requests, change it up by asking group members to write their requests down and email them to the group later. This will help eliminate one opportunity for a drainer to take over.
- The level of the person's needs may require professional care that your group is not equipped to offer. If this is the case, connect with a church leader to help facilitate next steps for help.

With all of these examples, use Paul's advice in Ephesians as your guide to the response.

> And be kind and compassionate to one another, forgiving one another, just as God also forgave you in Christ. (Eph. 4:32)

However, that doesn't mean that there shouldn't be healthy boundaries in place. Shepherds have a sheep pen where only the sheep may gather. Jesus gave us this picture in John 10:

> "Truly I tell you, anyone who doesn't enter the sheep pen by the gate but climbs in some other way is a thief and a robber. The

one who enters by the gate is the shepherd
of the sheep." (vv. 1–2)

There are times when our families must come first.
And there will be times when a toxic member of the group
may need to step out of the group to receive professional
counseling before returning. Hurting people hurt people,
and one person can destroy a group if not dealt with in a
biblical and honest manner. If this is the case, it's always
best to bring a pastor or church staff member into the
situation as soon as possible. The process laid out in
Matthew 18:15–17 should be followed in a small group
just like in a church.

> "If your brother sins against you, go and
> rebuke him in private. If he listens to you,
> you have won your brother. But if he won't
> listen, take one or two others with you, so
> that by the testimony of two or three wit-
> nesses every fact may be established. If
> he doesn't pay attention to them, tell the
> church. If he doesn't pay attention even to
> the church, let him be like a Gentile and a
> tax collector to you."

A group member should only be asked to leave the
group after all attempts have been made to restore him
to health and fellowship.

My Experience

I dislike conflict, so confronting someone in my group is extremely painful for me. I would much rather shove it under a rug and hope that everything will work out in the end than take steps to head it off early. This non-approach to conflict has cost our groups and relationships several times through the years. Because of this, I have found that bringing someone else into the conversation when there is potential for conflict is beneficial. We all have blind spots in our leadership and occasionally need someone to shine a light on them.

QUESTIONS TO THINK ABOUT

1. What stood out the most to you from this chapter?

_____

_____

2. Do you agree with the leader only talking 30 percent of the time? Why or why not?

_____

_____

3. Are you comfortable with some silence in your group? How can you use silence to help the discussion?

_____

_____

4. Which "D" have you spotted in your groups in the past? Which will be the most difficult for you to lead well?

_____

_____

5. What are a few things you can do to help that person integrate better into the life of the group?

_____

_____

CHAPTER 8

Showing Biblical Hospitality

I can't count the number of times I've heard someone say, "I just don't have the spiritual gift of hospitality." I have even said it about myself. I don't know about you, but when I think of someone gifted in hospitality, I picture Martha Stewart on the cover of a glossy magazine. Everything in the house is beautifully laid out and impossibly perfect. That's just not me.

It's probably not you either, but that's okay. You don't need perfectly prepped centerpieces and fresh-squeezed juices to fulfill the Bible's vision for hospitality. The "why" of hospitality is more valuable than the "what." While external expressions of hospitality—a clean house, good food, and nice people—are important to creating a complete small group experience, it goes much deeper than that.

Paul lays out the basis of biblical hospitality for us in Romans.

> Let love be without hypocrisy. Detest evil; cling to what is good. Love one another deeply as brothers and sisters. Outdo one another in showing honor. Do not lack diligence in zeal; be fervent in the Spirit; serve the Lord. Rejoice in hope; be patient in affliction; be persistent in prayer. Share with the saints in their needs; pursue hospitality. Bless those who persecute you; bless and do not curse. Rejoice with those who rejoice; weep with those who weep. (Rom. 12:9–15)

We can see clearly here that hospitality is not only for people with the full range of home canning equipment, but something to be pursued by every Christ follower. All the actions and attitudes laid out in this passage were exemplified by the life of Jesus. Because He first loved deeply, honored extravagantly, and remained patient always, we are commanded to do the same. First Peter 4:9 further commands us to "Be hospitable to one another without complaining." These selfless acts are to be done with joy.

To understand why that is, we need to first understand what hospitality really is. While there are certain acts like making the casserole or opening your home that are indicative of hospitality, the characteristic itself has a deeper meaning and implication than these actions.

The word *hospitality* comes from the combination of two words: *love* and *stranger*. Literally, hospitality is the love of strangers. This is a powerful description of what the gospel is. When we were strangers and aliens, God took us in. When we were without a home and family, God brought us into His. When we were without hope in the world, God adopted us as His children. In the ultimate act of hospitality, God provided a way to welcome us through the death of Jesus Christ. God is perfectly hospitable, and therefore, hospitality is a characteristic built into the spiritual DNA of all who have experienced His divine hospitality.

> The word *hospitality* comes from the combination of two words: *love* and *stranger*. Literally, hospitality is the love of strangers.

Hospitality, then, is that characteristic that compels us to put aside our own interests, to lay down our own desires, and to place the needs of others ahead of our own, just as Jesus did with His life and death.

We can see examples of welcoming strangers and outsiders throughout the Bible.

> "'For I was hungry and you gave me something to eat; I was thirsty and you gave me something to drink; I was a stranger and you took me in.'" (Matt. 25:35)

> Don't neglect to show hospitality, for by doing this some have welcomed angels as guests without knowing it. (Heb. 13:2)

> "You must not oppress a resident alien; you yourselves know how it feels to be a resident alien because you were resident aliens in the land of Egypt." (Exod. 23:9)

Because God has shown us hospitality through the gift of His Son, Jesus Christ, we are to mirror that through our love for one another. This is essential to the gospel, and I don't know a better opportunity than in a small group of believers. So how do we practically live this out in our small group?

Be open to inviting strangers into the group. This is not the case for every small group; a few groups, like recovery groups, will need to stay closed for accountability and confidentiality. But most groups can be open to offering community to those who need it most. The expectation of group members inviting others into the group will need to be discussed at the start of the group life and made a part of the group covenant.

Remember that everything speaks. Walt Disney was famous for insisting that everything in his amusement parks sends signals about what the organization values. This applied all the way down to how the pavement changed between the different sections of the park. He said, "You can get information about a changing environment through the soles of your feet." Our hospitality in the small group starts with how the environment speaks to the new member. Was there a smiling face at the door? Did group members welcome the new person in? Did the condition of the house show we care about the comfort of our guests?

Be the first to serve and the last to eat. In his book, *Leaders Eat Last*, Simon Sinek makes the case that good leadership is the willingness to put the needs of the people before your own. He says, "Great leaders truly care about those they are privileged to lead and understand that the true cost of the leadership privilege comes at the expense of self-interest."[2] This can be as literal as allowing your group members to always get their food first, or it can be a mind-set expressed by making yourself physically and emotionally available when they are in a crisis.

Pray consistently for the group. Extravagant hospitality begins with seeking God's favor and provision on the group members. Prayer sets the stage for life-changing moments to occur through the action of love toward friends and strangers. As you build your group roster, take time each day to pray for each member by name. Once the group has started, occasionally send a text or direct message to a group member of the same sex to let them know you are praying for them that day. Our love of friends and strangers alike will set the foundation for a gospel-centered small group. For the small group leader, hospitality is not just an act to be performed; it is a posture to be assumed.

My Experience

Hospitality is definitely not one of my spiritual gifts. Fortunately for our groups, it is one of my wife's. She is amazing with people and seems to always know how to create the perfect setting for our groups. If you struggle in this area, look for a cohost who can help fill in that gap—but never let this be an excuse to carry around an unhospitable attitude.

QUESTIONS TO THINK ABOUT

1. What stood out the most to you in this chapter?

_____

_____

2. Do you think you have the gift of hospitality? Why or why not?

_____

_____

3. How important do you feel showing gospel-centered hospitality to your group is?

_____

_____

4. Will your group be open to inviting "strangers" in?

_____

_____

5. What are a few practical ways you can show hospitality to your group this week?

_____

_____

CHAPTER 9

Practicing Genuine Authenticity

t is sometimes hard to know what is real in our society. We live in a world where we judge ourselves with comparisons to viral hashtags and perfect Instagram filters. Everyone's best life is on full display 24/7.

Ironically, those Instagram and Facebook posts signal the presence of authenticity. "I'm being authentic by letting you in to what's going on in my real life." But we all know that's a fake authenticity. There is a near-paralyzing fear that comes with true authenticity. The thoughts bombard us every time we start to grow in relationship with others. If people only knew . . .

- The things I have done in my past
- My shortcomings as a spouse
- My failures as a parent

- My private thoughts
- Sin based in my insecurities

The beautiful and freeing truth of true authenticity is that being open and vulnerable to a group of people doesn't require walking in perfection; it requires walking in confession. Scripture lays it out this way in 1 John:

> Now this is the message we have heard from Him and declare to you: God is light, and there is absolutely no darkness in Him. If we say, "We have fellowship with Him," yet we walk in darkness, we are lying and are not practicing the truth. But if we walk in the light as He Himself is in the light, we have fellowship with one another, and the blood of Jesus His Son cleanses us from all sin. If we say, "We have no sin," we are deceiving ourselves, and the truth is not in us. If we confess our sins, He is faithful and righteous to forgive us our sins and to cleanse us from all unrighteousness. (1 John 1:5–9 HCSB)

Our natural reaction to sin is to run and hide in darkness, but the power of the gospel frees us to come out into the light. Because of the blood of Jesus, we don't have to be afraid of confessing our sin—not because we don't sin or our sin doesn't have consequences, but because through the gospel, we know we are forgiven of our sins. That allows us to confess without self-justification. Now we can confess to one another not just so we will receive forgiveness from one another, but so that the forgiveness Jesus has already given to us can be pronounced again and again in our communities.

The picture is found in James 5:16: "Therefore, confess your sins to one another and pray for one another, so that you may be healed. The urgent request of a righteous person is very powerful in its effect" (HCSB).

This verse is transparency at its best. It's a picture of someone who, convinced of the limitless grace and promised forgiveness of Jesus, confesses their sin. They lay themselves open and bare before others, not expecting shame or guilt, but instead expecting healing. It's a crucial step on the road to holiness, but that's just the thing—it's one step on the road. It's not an end in itself.

The gospel both enables us to be truly transparent and compels us toward a greater end that lies beyond transparency. We confess to one another not so we can be real with one another; we confess to one another because we have a desire to be made holy. To be healed. To stop sinning. And we are responsible and even blessed for aiding one another on that journey. James continues on in verses 19 and 20:

> My brothers, if any among you strays from
> the truth, and someone turns him back, let

him know that whoever turns a sinner from the error of his way will save his life from death and cover a multitude of sins. (HCSB)

The work of Jesus makes confession and repentance more beautiful than burdensome. We can share "below the line of shame" because we already know we are so broken that Jesus had to die for us. But we also know we are so loved that He was willing to die for us.

> The gospel both enables us to be truly transparent and compels us toward a greater end that lies beyond transparency.

The only way for a small group to embrace this power of healing is for the leader to model and practice it from the beginning. Here are a few practices that will help your group live in the freedom that comes from embracing authenticity.

Be willing to lead the way. A good practice of facilitation is to ask questions and let the group answer before giving your opinion. But when you're leading with a personal-type question, it's always good to model vulnerability by going first with your experience. This will help the group feel at ease about opening up and set the culture of confession from the beginning.

As you model authenticity, be careful to keep a respectful and honoring attitude toward others in the group. We can sometimes unintentionally hurt people by downplaying their opinions or beliefs during a frank conversation. An example of this is when politics are brought up during the discussion. Most political conversations should be discussed outside of the group time, because nothing divides a group quicker than taking sides on a political issue.

Be prepared before the group meeting. Go over the study for the group time and mentally prepare your answers for each question. This will help you feel more confident about sharing something vulnerable to the group. The group members will then follow your approach to the openness of the discussion.

Ease into the personal questions. Especially if this is a new group. It will take time to build the relationships and trust necessary for open conversation. A group that "goes there" too quickly will scare off members who need more time. Give your group the opportunity to form relationships before asking them to get too personal.

Keep the focus on Jesus and grace. Continue to point the group back to the message of the cross. Authenticity will come when we think about the amazing love Christ showed us by laying down His life for our sin. When the conversation turns to judgment, gently remind the group that we are all sinners in need of a risen Savior.

There may be times when a group member will use
the guise of "being authentic" to share grievances with
another person, or use offensive language during the
discussion. Your ultimate response to this may differ
slightly according to the spiritual level of the offending
person but should be addressed quickly with concern for
the group as a whole. Be prepared to redirect back to the
main topic with something like, "Thank you for sharing,
but let's not lose focus on our main discussion."

That should be enough to get the group back on
track, but if the issue is ongoing, you will need to
address it directly with the group member outside of
group time—especially if the member is a more seasoned believer and has influence within the group. He
or she needs to be reminded what the group is about and
asked to partner with you in helping keep the discussions positive and focused on helping people take their
spiritual next steps. A few extreme situations may need
a pastor or church leader to step in for mediation and
correction, but that level of problem in a group is very
rare in my experience.

Make prayer an integral part of the group experience.
It's easy to spend too much time on the discussion segment and not have room for prayer at the end. It's also
easy to have the prayer time hijacked by too much time
spent on the prayer requests. If we're not careful, that
time can be used for thinly disguised gossip. Prayer as a
group is important. Communal prayer is demonstrated

throughout Scripture, but the key is having actual, focused prayer.

Focus the prayer time first on what God has shown you through the study. Ask God to help the group members live out the principles He has shown them in the Scriptures. Then, take a few minutes to lift to God individual needs of the group, also applying the principles from Scripture to those needs.

You can be creative for how you handle requests. If you see the prayer request time going long, ask members to write them down, and then divide up the requests with the group. You can share both requests and answered prayers through email or on a private Facebook page. You can also put the requests in a "requests" jar and then transfer them to an "answered" jar as those needs are met. This will give the group a great visual that God does still answer prayer.

James said confession leads to prayer, and prayer leads to healing. In order for group members to get to healing, there has to be concerted prayer. This sometimes means the group time may need to be interrupted to pray for a hurting member in the moment of confession. Be open to where the Spirit is leading the group.

My Experience

My first men's group experience was almost my last. I knew none of the men that morning when we were asked by the leader to go around the table and confess our biggest struggle. That experience kept me from having anything to do with men's groups for several years. True authenticity can take time to develop, and some discussions are best handled one-on-one outside the group time.

QUESTIONS TO THINK ABOUT

1. What stood out the most to you in this chapter?

2. What worries you the most about being completely authentic with your group?

3. Have you experienced true authenticity with a group or another individual? If yes, how did that experience help your spiritual growth?

4. How can you help your small group achieve real authenticity?

CHAPTER 10

Developing Honoring Service

One church in which I served sat in an interesting place geographically. The side of the main road where the building sat was quickly gentrifying: grand homes were being restored and flipped for big dollars, and the neighborhood was becoming a desirable place to live again.

However, directly across the street was a different picture. Drugs and gangs were destroying families, and the crime rate was one of the highest in the entire city. While we felt comfortable being on the "right side of the street," we knew we couldn't just sit and watch the pain occurring on the other side of our windows. This tension eventually led to a 24/7 Dream Center with a food pantry, dental clinic, after-school tutoring, free legal services, and much more, but it started with a handful of small groups who decided to love on and adopt a dying community. Those groups would consistently show up every month to walk the streets and offer basic needs, like light bulbs, to as many houses as would open their doors. That community continues to change because those first few small groups decided to serve.

Before we try to find ways for our small group to change our community, we first have to understand why we serve in the first place. We serve because Christ has already served us. We are the man hurt and broken on the side of the road, and Jesus is the good Samaritan long before we are to be the Samaritan for someone else. Jesus put it this way to His disciples in Matthew:

> "You know that the rulers of the Gentiles lord it over them, and those in high positions act as tyrants over them. It must not be like that among you. On the contrary, whoever wants to become great among you must be your servant, and whoever wants to be first among you must be your slave; just as the Son of Man did not come to be served, but to serve, and to give his life as a ransom for many." (20:25–28)

Serving starts with the good news that Jesus saw us, served us, and sacrificed Himself for us. Once we comprehend that we are broken and needy first, we can truly begin to serve the broken and needy around us.

So, how do we begin mirroring the gospel of serving with our small group? Here are five steps to help your group live out gospel-centered service.

> We serve because Christ has already served us.

Serve Your Group First

If you expect your small group to become a serving group, you have to first model servant leadership for your group members. Paul gave these instructions to the church in Philippi:

> Do nothing out of selfish ambition or conceit, but in humility consider others as more important than yourselves. Everyone should look out not only for his own interests, but also for the interests of others. Adopt the same attitude as that of Christ Jesus. (Phil. 2:3–5)

Jesus set the ultimate example of servanthood in His relationship with His disciples and ultimately all of us on the cross. As you begin your group, make sure you serve group members unconditionally and tangibly. There are no expectations attached with true servanthood.

Here are a few tangible ways you can serve your group members:

- Offer to watch their kids so they can have a date night.
- Bring meals to the family when there is a crisis or a new baby.
- Randomly show up on a Saturday and wash their car.
- Mow their lawn while they are on vacation.
- Surprise them with their favorite coffee or tea at church.

Empower Group Members to Serve the Group

Even the disciples had to eventually turn over ownership to their quickly multiplying group.

In those days, as the disciples were increasing in number, there arose a complaint by the Hellenistic Jews against the Hebraic Jews that their widows were being overlooked in the daily distribution. The Twelve summoned the whole company of the disciples and said, "It would not be right for us to give up preaching the word of God to wait on tables. Brothers and sisters, select from among you seven

men of good reputation, full of the Spirit
and wisdom, whom we can appoint to
this duty. But we will devote ourselves to
prayer and to the ministry of the word."
(Acts 6:1–4)

The disciples discovered a need within their growing group and released and empowered members to fill it
with their gifts. You are discipling your group members
by helping them discover their spiritual gifts to utilize
within the group. Here are a few roles to give away:

- Hosting the group
- Providing the food
- Facilitating the discussion
- Handling the prayer time
- Planning events
- Planning missional opportunities

Ask the group members to take an online spiritual
gifts test and spend part of a group meeting talking about
where group members' gifts and passions are. Then
release them to own that portion of the group experience
(example in the Resources Appendix).

Serve Together in the Church

There are always opportunities for groups to serve
somewhere together in the church. A classroom needs

to be painted. The church landscaping needs extra care on a Saturday. The student ministry needs more bodies for an event. Kids ministry volunteers need a break for a few weeks. Take a few minutes at a group meeting to brainstorm ideas where the group can come alongside a ministry within the church. Make sure to check in with church leadership before taking on a project. Some ministry areas, like youth and children, will need background checks and interviews before new people can serve in them.

Serve Together in the Community

Just like the small groups at my church saw a need across the street and met it, there are needs around your community. A single mom needs her yard mowed. An under-resourced local school needs more supplies for the teachers. A local fire or police station could use encouragement through a batch of cookies. Whatever you do may seem small or insignificant, but you have to start somewhere. The only way a community will be transformed is through one block at a time, by one small group at a time.

Serve Together in the World

Nothing bonds a group together faster than taking a short-term missions trip together. If your church does not offer them, check with Christian organizations in your area who may sponsor independent trips. Jesus told us in the Great Commission to "Go, therefore, and make disciples of *all nations*" (Matt. 28:19, emphasis added). Our mission does not end at our country's borders.

Serving together as a group has to be an intentional effort from the first group meeting. Begin sowing the seeds of being a serving group with your posture and language as a leader.

My Experience

My default mode is to control everything about the group experience. Part of it is wanting everything to be done well, and part is not wanting to burden anyone with a task. I have had to become comfortable with not everything being done the way I would do it, and not being afraid to challenge group members to take ownership. I have learned that most people will not know how to help until you give them a way to help.

QUESTIONS TO THINK ABOUT

1. What stood out the most to you in this chapter?

_____

_____

2. Have you had a group or another individual serve you without obligation? If yes, how did that make you feel?

_____

_____

3. What are a few tangible ways you could start serving your group members?

_____

_____

4. What are a few needs in your church or community that your group could meet right now?

_____

_____

5. What global missions opportunities are available to your group?

_____

_____

CHAPTER 11

Being on Mission

E very small group needs a reason for existence. Why should we carve out more time in our busy lives to spend it with people we might barely know? For most people and groups that reason is the desire for community. We desire friendship, and that is a good thing.

We all need community. In fact, we were designed by God to be in community. You can see it modeled for us with the perfect relationship of the Trinity in Genesis.

> Then God said, "Let Us make man in Our image, according to Our likeness. They will rule the fish of the sea, the birds of the sky, the livestock, all the earth, and the creatures that crawl on the earth." (Gen. 1:26 HCSB)

We then see it prayed for by Jesus with His final prayer before His death on the cross:

> "May they all be one, as You, Father, are in Me and I am in You. May they also be one in Us, so the world may believe You sent Me." (John 17:21 HCSB)

Community is important, but a problem arises when community is the destination of the group. A small group that gathers strictly around the desire to make friends will live or die on the strength of those relationships. If those relationships begin to shift or separate, so will the group. Without the imperative of being on mission, community is fragile.

Like all aspects of God's creation, our relationships have been broken by sin. In our sinfulness, we use other people instead of live in God-honoring community with them. But when we believe the gospel, our relationships begin to be reshaped. We, together, are meant to help each other follow Jesus more closely and in so doing to extend the gospel into all the world. This is our mission. This is the redeemed version of community—it's relationships that are centered on seeing the mission of God come to pass first in our own hearts, and eventually in the world.

We can look at the life of Jesus to see how community was used as the foundation for mission. As we saw in Genesis 1:26, Jesus had this perfect community with the Trinity, but chose to not only leave home, but to leave heaven on a mission to die for those He came to reach. Jesus was the first and greatest missionary of all history! John testified to the fullness of Jesus' mission in John 1:

> Indeed, we have all received grace upon grace from his fullness, for the law was given through Moses; grace and truth came through Jesus Christ. No one has ever seen God. The one and only Son, who is himself God and is at the Father's side—he has revealed him. (vv. 16–18)

Jesus left His community to come to Earth, to realign our priorities, and to make us citizens of a new kingdom. Because of sin, our priorities are broken, but the gospel puts them back in line. The truth of this gospel was the sole mission of Jesus' life on Earth.

When Pilate questioned who He was, Jesus replied, "You say that I'm a king . . . I was born for this, and I have come into the world for this: to testify to the truth. Everyone who is of the truth listens to my voice" (John 18:37). Jesus was born to share this truth.

We can see clearly why living out the mission of Jesus is related to the gospel. After all, the final instructions of Jesus before He ascended into heaven were centered around this mission—that His followers should "Go, therefore, and make disciples of all nations, baptizing them in the name of the Father and of the Son and of the Holy Spirit, teaching them to observe everything I have commanded you" (Matt. 28:19–20).

And as you align your group around this gospel-centered mission of Jesus, remember that we had to hear the good news before we could share the good news. We had to be brought to life by the message before we could be its messengers. What this means practically is that we have to be open to living out the gospel in our group by inviting those who need the gospel the most.

With time of living it out, this missional way of looking at our world becomes a natural outflow of what the gospel has produced in our lives. We desire deeply for others to experience what we have in our life-giving community. Helping group members see their world through this new missional lens will slowly move them beyond just the desire for friendships.

Here are a few things you can do to help your group be on mission from the beginning:

Set the expectation early that the group is open to new people who might need what the group can offer. Do this with the covenant at the first meeting that sets the foundation for the group's existence. Covenant together that you will look for and invite those who need the good news of the gospel.

Include studies that help the group understand the mission of Jesus. Groups will drift toward their favorite subjects, but a balanced curriculum map will consistently bring the group back to the heart of the gospel. There is an example of a balanced curriculum plan in the Resources Appendix.

Take part in at least one missional activity every quarter. Again, include this expectation in the covenant so members know from the beginning that the goal of the group is to be outward focused. Look for opportunities with organizations already making a difference in your community. Your church may have a list of organizations they have partnered with in the past. These events aren't the end goal, but they are a great launching pad to move people into living missional lives.

End each group meeting by praying for opportunities to live out the gospel that week. The mission is not just a group activity. Each one of us has a mandate to live as missionaries in our daily lives. Every person we come across is an opportunity to follow Jesus in His mission to share the truth to a hurting and dying world.

Remember that community is an important piece of group life, but community should not be the destination. Being on mission should result from biblical community. Jesus does not want us to gather so we can remain gathered. We are gathered to be sent out.

> "You are the salt of the earth. But if the salt should lose its taste, how can it be made salty? It's no longer good for anything but to be thrown out and trampled

on by men. "You are the light of the world.
A city situated on a hill cannot be hidden.
No one lights a lamp and puts it under a
basket, but rather on a lampstand, and it
gives light for all who are in the house. In
the same way, let your light shine before
men, so that they may see your good works
and give glory to your Father in heaven."
(Matt. 5:13–16 HCSB)

All of Jesus' illustrations assume that we are in the
world, impacting all the cultures we find there.

My Experience

My groups will always be open to new people. This
can become a challenge when space is an issue, or the
study is more in-depth, but I always want our group
members to be thinking about someone they need to
invite for community. Staying open as a group sets the
tone for always being on mission.

QUESTIONS TO THINK ABOUT

1. What stood out the most to you from this chapter?

_____

_____

2. What does it look like for you personally to be on mission for Christ?

_____

_____

3. How can you help your small group members think more missionally?

_____

_____

4. What practical steps can you take this week to move your group toward a gospel-centered mission?

_____

_____

CHAPTER 12

Developing a Bible Study

I am not much of a handyman. When something
breaks at our house, my first instinct is to call in
a professional who knows what he's doing. What I
have discovered (several hundreds of dollars in service
bills later) is that often the only thing stopping me from
doing the repair job myself is having the right tools. The
correct wrench and socket set can save a lot of pain, time,
and money.

The same principle is true for choosing and leading
a transformative Bible study with your small group. An
essential tool of a gospel-centered small group is choosing a study that always points back to the centrality of
the gospel of Jesus.

An effective Bible study will always, first and fore-
most, show Christ through the narrative of the text.
Tim Keller says of this truth: "You can't really reach and

restructure the affections of the heart unless you point through the biblical principles to the beauty of Jesus himself, showing clearly how the particular truth in your text can be practiced only through faith in the work of Christ."[3]

We can see throughout Paul's writing in the New Testament that he continually points to Christ as the source of our salvation and sanctification.

> When I came to you, brothers and sisters, announcing the mystery of God to you, I did not come with brilliance of speech or wisdom. I decided to know nothing among you except Jesus Christ and him crucified. (1 Cor. 2:1–2)

Keller says of Paul's ministry: "At the time Paul was writing, the only Scripture to preach from was what we now call the Old Testament. Yet even when preaching from these texts Paul 'knew nothing' but Jesus . . ."[4]

As we lead a study, we should also note Paul's pattern of teaching in the epistles of "believe, become, behave." This is the work of the gospel—that we are reminded of what we believe; that because of the gospel we believe we have become something different; and then as a result of the new creation we have become, our behavior begins to change. In our study of the Bible, we must keep this order in mind.

Bible Study Tools

As you prepare for a Bible study, there are a few tools that can help you feel more confident as you work through the text.

Bible Commentary

Commentaries are written by well-known and respected theologians, and aid in the study of Scripture by providing explanation and interpretation of biblical texts. Three commentary sets I've found helpful are:

- The New American Commentary
- The Holman New Testament Commentary
- The Holman Old Testament Commentary

Bible Concordance

A concordance can help you locate important Bible references by indexing every verse that contains a particular word. This will help you assemble a list of Bible references on almost any topic.

Bible Encyclopedia

These are often massive in their scope. They present, in an organized fashion, page after page of information about Bible times and customs, important historical periods, and persons.

Bible Dictionary

Arranged much like a typical English dictionary, it contains valuable entries that will help you learn the proper pronunciation of obscure biblical words. A Bible dictionary will also provide information on important biblical persons and summaries of various books of the Bible as well as other important teachings.

Online Study Tools

There are thousands of resources currently available online at no cost to you. Spend a little time searching for Bible study resources and bookmark your favorites.

Video-Enhanced Studies

There are now many Bible studies that have videos to go along with the study guides. These videos are normally recordings of the study's author to help the group get the discussion started with a short teaching on the topic. They can vary anywhere from five minutes to forty-five minutes—or longer.

Video-enhanced studies can be a great curriculum tool for small group leaders. They free the leader up to focus on the discipleship conversations while making sure the group is getting doctrinally sound teaching from talented teachers you can trust.

Widespread use of Internet has made the video delivery easier. Instead of having to purchase a DVD, the group can stream it straight from a site like smallgroup.com to the living room television or computer.

Video-enhanced studies can make the experience feel like it's plug-and-play, but like any other discipleship tool, there are a few things the leader should still do to make it a better experience for the group.

Watch the video ahead of time.

A good leader is always one step ahead in the process so she knows how to steer the discussion in the right direction. Watching the video and going over the questions before the meeting helps you know where the finish line should be for the meeting. We always want the truth of God's Word to be the landing spot for the discussion. That will be easier to achieve if the leader is prepared for the topic.

Pretest the tech.

We can distract from the group experience by just assuming the video will work. Technical issues will occasionally happen no matter what, but testing it every time before the meeting will help make those awkward moments rare. If you are streaming the video, make sure your Internet speed is fast enough to handle the video size. Plan to always stream the video completely through before the meeting to watch for potential glitches.

Allow the group to process the teaching.

If a leader has done his homework and prewatched the video, then he is already familiar with the material and ready to dive right into the discussion. The rest of the group, however, will need a few moments to process what they watched. It's okay to let the first couple of questions hang in the air while everyone is still taking it in.

Study the Bible, not the teacher.

A good video-enhanced study will lead the group to examine the Bible for answers, but it will be tempting to only discuss the best quotes from the teaching. The leader will need to always press the group to dig further into Scripture and not just rely on the video. That's why it's so important to have a study guide to go along with the video teaching. It's even better for each group member to have his or her own study guide to take notes and dig deeper on their own time.

Leave time after the video for discussion.

One of the most important pieces of a successful Bible study is time management. A good leader should always keep one eye on the clock and know when to move the group to the next segment of the study. If the group spends too much time on the icebreakers, and the video is thirty minutes or longer, there will not be enough time to study the Scripture behind the teaching and discuss how to apply it to their lives. With longer videos, it may be helpful for group members to have access to them ahead of time to watch on their own before the meeting.

A Balanced Curriculum Plan

I have a go-to low-carb eating plan I turn to whenever I sense the extra pounds coming back on. The diet includes mostly eating eggs and black beans every morning. I will be honest, before starting this plan, I was not a raving fan of eggs and black beans. But what I had not yet discovered was how creative you can get when you are desperate. I knew the only way I would last longer than one week on this diet was by coming up with a variety of ways to prepare eggs and beans. However, no matter how many ways I spice it, I am still only eating eggs and beans. Every day. That might be great for the short-term gain, but it's not exactly a balanced, healthy diet.

In the same way, your group members will not be their healthiest without a balanced spiritual diet. Our goal should be to create mature disciples who make disciples, and the best way to achieve this is by offering your group a well-rounded discipleship curriculum plan to follow throughout the year. Here are two reasons to consider a progressive plan:

1. It will drive members toward spiritual maturity.

The author of Hebrews compels us to seek maturity in Hebrews 6:1: "Therefore, leaving the elementary message about the Messiah, let us go on to maturity . . ." (HSCB). J. Oswald Sanders said the correct sense of the verb in this passage is, "Let us continue progressing toward maturity."[5] In other words, maturity will not occur overnight. There is not one event or moment—or Bible study—that will make us mature Christians. It happens slowly through a growing knowledge of Jesus and Scripture, and the way to get there is through intentional study after intentional study with a group of believers.

2. It will help assure sound theology.

Groupthink can quickly lead to bad theology. Doctrinally sound content will help keep the group on the path toward truth. A well-written study can provide a theology fence for the discussion to stay in. This is why LifeWay has developed a balanced discipleship plan for group leaders to follow. Throughout the course of a year, you can choose studies from eight categories that will ultimately move members toward spiritual maturity. You can find this plan in the Resources Appendix.

No matter what type of study you use, one of the best things you can do for your group is to simply, and many times explicitly, bring them back to the truth of the gospel. The question, "What does the gospel say about this issue?" should be well worn in our small groups. When we ask that question again and again, we will find that the gospel has much to say indeed about the varied and many issues we will discuss.

My Experience

I discovered early on the importance of making sure the study is easy-to-lead and practical for the whole group. We decided to take our couples group through a quick study of a very short devotional book. The entire book was ninety-six pages long. As I looked around the room to start the first discussion, not a single person made eye contact with me. I knew immediately that no one had read the book. They could have finished it in the time most of them took to drive to group, but it didn't happen. That was the last book study our groups have done.

QUESTIONS TO THINK ABOUT

1. What stood out the most to you from this chapter?

_____

_____

2. Do you agree that having a gospel-centered Bible study in your group is crucial? Why or why not?

_____

_____

3. What components should a good Bible study have?

_____

_____

4. What are the pros and cons with video-enhanced studies? Would these be helpful in your group?

_____

_____

5. What category of study should your group start with on the discipleship plan?

_____

_____

SECTION IV

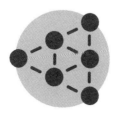

Multiplying Your Small Group

CHAPTER 13

Multiplication Instead of Addition

After we have experienced genuine biblical community in a small group, the thought of anyone leaving that community is very hard. We want to keep what we are experiencing for as long as we can. But the mandate to continue making disciples is clear. The only way to make room for more people to start their personal discipleship journey is by creating new groups for them.

We can see the progression from addition to multiplication with the early church. Acts 2:47 says, "Every day the Lord *added* to their number those who were being saved" (emphasis added).

For an initial period of your small group, you will add new group members to the existing group. This will work

137

until the group is at a critical mass and space becomes an issue. You may be able to subdivide for a time, but to make room for new people, incremental addition will have to change to multiplication.

We see this critical change in the early church at Acts 6:7 (HCSB): "So the preaching about God flourished, the number of the disciples in Jerusalem *multiplied* greatly, and a large group of priests became obedient to the faith" (emphasis added). They were experiencing exponential growth and had to change their systems and mind-set to best minister through that growth. Their addition had changed to multiplication.

> The only way to make room for more people to start their personal discipleship journey is by creating new groups for them.

Multiplying your small group will take time. It may take a few semesters of growth before your group is ready to birth a new group, but the key is to prepare early for that eventual new group launch.

Developing a Secondary Leader

The first step toward launching a new group for new people is identifying someone in your group to be a secondary leader or apprentice. This will be someone who is developing into a mature believer and is showing signs of taking ownership in the group. He may not recognize the leadership potential in himself yet, so you will need to affirm those gifts you see.

I use these five steps to develop secondary leaders in my groups:

Step 1: I do. You watch. We talk.

After I have approached my potential secondary leader and asked him to pray about taking more ownership in the group, I will encourage him to watch how I facilitate the next group meeting. We then arrange time (possibly after the meeting) to connect and talk about his observations. This begins the process of modeling what I want him to do.

Step 2: I do. You help. We talk.

If my potential secondary leader is ready to move on, I ask him to facilitate a portion of the discussion at the next group meeting. I give him the questions several days ahead of time so he can be prepared to navigate through the transitions and potential answers. We again meet afterward to discuss the experience and next steps.

Step 3: You do. I help. We talk.

The next step for my secondary leader is to facilitate a majority of the discussion while I help where needed. I may still lead through the prayer time at this stage until he is comfortable handling it himself. We again meet afterward to discuss the experience. If this step goes well, he should be ready to own the next one.

Step 4: You do. I watch. We talk.

It is now time for my secondary leader to facilitate the entire group experience while I observe as a participant in the group. This can be a difficult experience for me as a leader because that secondary leader will probably lead differently than I would. That's okay and, in fact, it's healthy. It's now time to turn over the reins and begin the process with someone new.

Step 5: You do. Someone else watches.

This process will eventually lead to birthing a new group. The secondary leader can either step out of the current group to lead a new group for new people, or I can turn the leadership of the current group over to him as I step out to launch the new group. The latter scenario can set the secondary leader up for success quicker. He is already comfortable with the current group, and I will be more prepared than him to start over.

Questions to Ask at the Meetings

An important key to developing a leader is the debrief meeting after each step. It will be tempting to skip it and move through the development process, but moving too quickly will set him up for potential failure. Here are five

questions to ask as you meet with your secondary leader
after each step of the process:

1. What did you observe?
2. How did this step make you feel?
3. What could be done better or differently next time?
4. What can I do to help you successfully
   lead through the next step?
5. How can I pray for you?

Celebrate the Birth

After each of my children were born, we celebrated
as a family. After all, it was a joyous event to welcome
a new life into the world! That event was worth a lot of
cake and ice cream. In the same way, we should celebrate
when a new leader is developed and a new small group is
birthed out of ours. It will be an adjustment to send off
a leader who has become an integral part of the group,
so the group members need to be reminded of the "why"
behind multiplying.

Many potential secondary leaders are hesitant to
step into the process because of the potential feeling of
loss when they leave. The birth of the new group does
not mean that fellowship with the leader stepping out
will cease to exist. A part of the celebration should be the
commitment to continue as a larger family meeting in

different locations. That could mean that the two groups continue to stay together for missional projects and fun activities outside the group time. You should also continue to meet occasionally with the new leader to coach them through leading the new group. This could start out as a weekly meeting and then switch to monthly as the new leader gains confidence.

Starting Over

The opportunity to start over will follow a successful birth of a new group. If you have handed over the reins of leadership to a secondary leader, this is your time to create another generation of disciples. Paul talked about creating multiple generations of disciples in 2 Timothy 2:2: "What you have heard from me in the presence of many witnesses, commit to faithful men who will be able to teach others also."

If you look at this passage closely, you see four generations of disciples represented. Paul is the first generation. He invested in the life of Timothy—that's generation two. Then Timothy was to commit what he learned from Paul to faithful men—that's our third generation. And the faithful men are meant to teach others also—generation number four.

The initial group and secondary leader was generation one for you. Through that leader and your next group, you will create generations of disciples who will carry the good news of the gospel to multiple others. This is how we will carry out the words of Jesus in the Great Commission.

Your small group can literally change the world. That fact is worth the effort and pain of multiplying and starting over.

> Your small group can literally change the world. That fact is worth the effort and pain of multiplying and starting over.

Knowing When to End the Group

There may come a time when you should consider ending the group instead of multiplying. If that time comes, it's important that you end the group well. Here are a few reasons a group may need to end:

- Group members are no longer growing spiritually. A group that has been together too long can grow stale and stop moving forward. If group members are no longer taking their next spiritual steps, it's time to consider disbanding.
- Group attendance has dwindled to just a few members. Keeping meetings consistent will be difficult with just a few people involved. If this is the case,

consider helping the remaining members find new groups.

- You are seeing signs of burning out as a leader. There may be a season where you need to step out of active leadership to take care of your emotional and spiritual health. Try to identify a secondary leader to take over the group before disbanding in this case.
- The group dynamic has become toxic. Groups will sometimes need to disband if gossip and discord has taken over the life of the group. Involve a pastor or church staff member in the ending to help the group heal after a bad experience.

My Experience

If I had not tapped someone on the shoulder to be my secondary leader, an amazing story may not have played out. A married couple had been attending the church for just a few months when they decided to join our small group. I quickly saw through the way the husband interacted with the group that he had a huge heart for people, so I asked him if he would facilitate the next group meeting while I was out of town. He hesitated and asked if he could sit down with me before committing.

He then shared with me his story of spending time in prison before coming to Christ several years ago. Even though God had completely turned his life around and he was now helping with a prison ministry, he was not sure if he was qualified to lead a small group in our church. I assured him he was and hoped he would lead the group while I was away. He not only led our group that next meeting but went on to eventually lead the small groups ministry at our church. You never know where that ask may lead.

QUESTIONS TO THINK ABOUT

1. What stood out the most to you from this chapter?

_____

_____

2. What is your biggest fear with the thought of multiplying your group?

_____

_____

3. Do you have someone in mind to approach as a potential secondary leader?

_____

_____

4. What is your next step toward developing a secondary leader?

_____

_____

5. Will you turn over the reins of your current group and start a new one when you multiply, or release a leader to start a new group?

_____

_____

6. What is the potential time line of birthing a new group out of your existing one?

_____

_____

CHAPTER 14

Staying Healthy as a Leader

t's important as a leader that we stay physically, mentally, and spiritually healthy. Leading a group can take a toll on our health if we are constantly pouring out and never being filled up. Churches and ministries are littered with former leaders who burned out because they were finding their identity by always doing for others instead of being who they are in their relationship with Christ.

There are even examples of great leaders reaching this point in the Bible. Moses had reached a tipping point with the people he was leading in Numbers 11.

> Moses heard the people, family after family, weeping at the entrance of their tents. The LORD was very angry; Moses was also

149

provoked. So Moses asked the Lord, "Why have you brought such trouble on your servant? Why are you angry with me, and why do you burden me with all these people? Did I conceive all these people? Did I give them birth so you should tell me, 'Carry them at your breast, as a nanny carries a baby,' to the land that you swore to give their fathers? Where can I get meat to give all these people? For they are weeping to me, 'Give us meat to eat!' I can't carry all these people by myself. They are too much for me. If you are going to treat me like this, please kill me right now if I have found favor with you, and don't let me see my misery anymore." (vv. 10–15)

Moses was carrying the burden for all of his people until he had had enough. He was finished. I have had a few of those moments through my ministry life. I always get to that point when I wrap my identity up in what I am doing for God, instead of who I am in God. Our ministry leadership should be a natural outflow of the work God is doing in us.

The Signs of Burnout

To avoid getting to the same dark place Moses was in, learn to recognize signs that you are spiritually empty. Peter Scazzero, in his book *Emotionally Healthy Spirituality*, lists a few signs of potential burnout I have found helpful to pay attention to in my life.[6]

You are using God to run from God. When we are running on empty spiritually, it's tempting to throw more time into what we think will please God. We manage to fill the void with more Christian activity.

You are ignoring the emotions of anger, sadness, and fear. We are afraid to express these feelings in our small group because they are somehow unbiblical. So we bottle them and put on the "Christian" face week after week.

You are dying to the wrong things. We are commanded to die to the sinful parts in our lives, but God did not call us to be miserable. A lot of Christians believe the more miserable you are, the better Christian you are.

You are denying the past's impact on the present. You may have had a tough childhood, or you may have been burned by a church or a small group experience in the past. But, no matter how much in the past those experiences are, they will influence actions we take today. You must recognize it and deal with it before you can move on.

You are doing for God instead of being with God. Our small group leadership becomes another check-off item for our spiritual list. We are forsaking the fuel for our ministry, which is time spent with God.

You are spiritualizing away conflict. Almost none of us are naturally good at handling conflict. You will eventually face conflict in your small group, and the tendency is to sweep it under the rug for the sake of group unity. The fact is: if it is not properly dealt with, it will eventually destroy you and your group.

You are covering over weakness, brokenness, and failure. As a leader, we want to present the best picture possible to our group. However, only when we become transparent and vulnerable will the group follow our leadership.

You are living without limits. Establishing healthy boundaries from the beginning is critical. As small group leaders, we want to help everyone in our group, but that is not possible all the time. Even Jesus did not heal everyone. There will be times when we need to step back from active leadership, and that's okay. We all need breaks to be ready for the next season of ministry.

Recognizing these signs of eventual burnout will not only help you stay spiritually strong but will also help the people you lead. We as leaders have to model for our group members the routine of daily prayer, consistent rest, and healthy relationships. The people we lead can only follow where we can take them.

Keep Relationship Boundaries

We start small groups as leaders because we love people and want to see them grow in their spiritual journey to be more like Christ, but it's impossible for a leader to be relationally close with everyone in his or her group. In fact, it's not healthy to attempt to nourish that many relationships. Trying to be everything to everyone will lead to burnout and missed expectations of the group members. As the group leader, you are not responsible to be every person in your group's best friend.

> It's impossible for a leader to be relationally close with everyone in his or her group.

In his book *Organic Community*, Joseph Myers describes the four patterns of belonging that every person can experience:

- Public belonging: This is where most small groups will start. You share common ground by attending the same church or living in the same neighborhood. There is a natural language between all the members of the group.

- Social belonging: This is the handful of people in the group you are not afraid to ask a favor from. They might

help a group member move to a new
house over the weekend. Or it may be a
group of guys from the group who own
motorcycles and like to ride together
twice a month.

• Personal belonging: These are relationships that grow out of social connections. You're willing to share a personal
prayer need outside group time with
these two or three people. They would
be considered close friends.

• Intimate belonging: In this space are
the one or two best friends who can
share the most personal joys and hurts.
This level of intimacy may not live
within the context of the group or even
the church, but everyone needs it.[7]

Small group leaders struggle under the weight of
expectations when they feel the pressure to exist at all
of these levels with everyone in their group. The reality
is that most people will not get past the social belonging level with their small group. An effective leader will
look for connections she can facilitate with like-minded
people in the group. She may never have a personal
belonging–level relationship with another member of the
group, but she may start the conversation that leads to
one between other group members.

We can promise to create environments where intimate community is possible, but we cannot guarantee it will happen. Your job as a leader is to offer the opportunity (the trellis) for healthy relationships to germinate (the vine) within the group; however, you are not responsible for forcing them to happen.

Keep Having Fun

The process of leading a small group can sometimes cause you to forget that it should be fun. Think about all the administration details you have to deal with.

- Where will the group meet?
- What day of the week will it meet?
- Who will be invited?
- Who will bring the food?
- How many members are gluten-free?
- What will the study be?

If you're not careful, your group can become a list of tasks to complete, not a community to be enjoyed. I believe your group can and should be fun, and here are a few reasons why:

Everyone likes fun! Quickly think through your top five memories in life. I bet most of them involved something fun. We are designed by God to enjoy life and the people around us. Why would we not include it in a weekly gathering of friends at our home?

156 LEADING SMALL GROUPS

Fun will help make group attendees come back. Most people will not return to a boring group—no matter how great the study is. I always judge how healthy a small group is by how much laughter there is during a group meeting. If you want people to go from visitors to members, make sure there's something to enjoy at the meeting.

Biblical community is supposed to be fun. You can see fun and laughter throughout the Bible. God's people constantly threw feasts to celebrate something God had done for them. That's another reason to always have good food at your group. Nothing brings people together faster than a great meal.

So, now we know there should be fun in our groups; but how do we go about making that happen? Here are three tips to get the fun back in:

Set the expectation for fun. You can kick off the group by planning something fun at the beginning. Plan to meet at a restaurant or go bowling for your first meeting. That will let everyone know this group is not just about the study. You can also spell it out in your group covenant at one of your first meetings. A line item can be something like: "This group will value having fun together."

Plan for fun. Set aside at least one meeting a quarter for just having fun. This could be going to a ball game, having a picnic, going river rafting, or having a game night. A healthy amount of competition can bond a group for a long time. You will also want to build time into the weekly meeting for fun. The first and last twenty minutes of the group time should be for just hanging out and enjoying each other's company.

Be a fun person to be around. The tone of fun starts with the leader. If you are too tied up in the details of pulling a group off every week, the group members will follow your lead. The fun starts with the hospitality displayed. Are you a smiling face at the door, or a stressed-out group host? A great attitude will set the atmosphere for the entire night and help keep you healthy as a leader.

My Experience

I burned out as a leader in 2004 and went through a period of anxiety and depression because of it. We had just moved to a new city to plant a church, and I was trying to do everything. My self-worth had become about my accomplishments and not about who I was in Christ. I now know firsthand the danger of not taking care of yourself spiritually, physically, and mentally. It took years to completely climb out of the dark hole and feel normal again. I hope this chapter can encourage you to attack that potential burnout before it attacks you.

QUESTIONS TO THINK ABOUT

1. What are steps you need to take to make sure you don't burn out as a leader?

_____

_____

2. Is it a relief to know you don't have to have an intimate relationship with everyone in the group?

_____

_____

3. What are steps you can take to make those personal and intimate relationships healthier?

_____

_____

4. How can you foster the opportunity for other members in your group to become personal and intimate friends with one another?

_____

_____

5. How can you make sure that your group stays fun? Is that easy or hard for you?

_____

_____

CHAPTER 15

Avoiding Group Killers

We've almost all been there at one point or another. You're excited to start a group or to be a part of a new group, but by week five or six, it's evident this may not last. By week eight or nine, you've stopped meeting, and then you're completely out of touch.

Even with as much planning and preparation as you will put into your small group, there will still be things that can kill the group off if not fixed or dealt with properly. It's discouraging and frustrating to be in a group that doesn't last, but I think we can avoid many of these group killers.

People Not Returning

As a leader, we hope that everyone invited loves the group and wants to be an active member. Unfortunately, that will not always be the case. We have never started a small group that had a 100 percent retention rate after the first couple of meetings. While there are a million reasons someone may try a group and not come back, there are a few common ones I have identified through the years.

The group has been together for a while and it's hard to see a place to fit in. No matter how open a group may seem, it can be difficult for a new person or couple to step into an existing group and feel comfortable. It's kind of like stepping into a new school in the middle of the year. There is already history and insider language among the group members. It will be easier for a newcomer if there is an already established relationship within the group and they are personally invited by that person.

There is no time invested in building community. Although a good Bible study is necessary for spiritual growth, most people do not come back for the study. They come back for the relationships. If your group is all about the study, it will limit the type and the number of people who will want to be involved.

There is no intentionality behind the studies chosen. People need an easy-to-follow spiritual path, and an intentional curriculum map helps them find it. A balance of biblical community and foundational studies are essential for discipleship.

The leader dominates the discussion. A leader who feels like he needs to dominate the discussion will eventually be the only group member.

The leader is unprepared for the group meeting. A leader who is not prepared is not leading. It doesn't have to be two hours of prep, but you should be at least one step ahead of the group. People will not return to a group that feels unorganized.

Relationship Breakups

Dealing with the aftermath of a broken relationship or friendship within a small group can be extremely tricky for a leader. It would be easy for group members to choose sides and splinter the group. The way the leader responds will set the direction of health and reconciliation for the people involved and for the entire group. Here are a few things you should do when a breakup happens:

Do not take sides. The leader's and members' roles are to love both people unconditionally. Taking sides will guarantee a split in the group. Of course, there are situations that arise when one person has clearly sinned against another, but most conflicts simply arise out of personality differences. Don't assume one person is in the wrong, and don't be afraid to elevate the conflict to a pastor or elder in the church.

Help them find new groups. If it's impossible for them to stay in the current group, work with the church leadership to find a group where they can begin to heal.

Be honest and open with the group. Rumors and speculation will destroy the trust of the group. If there are members who are personally affected by a situation, meet with them individually outside the normal group meeting time. It might be best to offer to meet with one of the church pastors at this point.

Allow God to strengthen relationships in the group. Satan wants nothing more than to destroy marriages and relationships, and he will use this opportunity to plant seeds of distrust. Use this time to help people in the group rededicate themselves to God and to each other. This is an ideal time to take the group through a good study about life together in the church.

Gossip

Gossip in a small group can seem to start out innocently enough. It may even initially appear as a benign prayer request that leads to side conversations over dessert. As gossip grows, it will lay the seeds of mistrust and eventually destroy the group. That is why it is so important to recognize it early and act quickly to stop it. Here are a few ideas for avoiding gossip in your group.

Include a confidentiality clause in the group covenant. Start the group in the right direction with gossip by declaring in the covenant that what is said in the group stays confident within the group. Being proactive with the potential of gossip will help group members feel more secure.

Recognize when a prayer need is turning into gossip. The prayer time can be seen as an opening to share thinly veiled grievances with other people. If you hear statements like, "Sharon is not living right again . . ." or, "I heard that Charles . . .", then act to head them off quickly. You may need to give guidelines of no specific names or situations in prayer requests if this becomes an issue.

Continually remind the members of the group's mission. When a small group loses sight of why it exists, it can turn into a social club where gossip is expected. Remind the group members that the group exists to help people take their next steps toward Christ; gossip turns that goal upside down.

Ask a member to leave the group as a last resort. Asking someone to step out of the group should always be the last option, but sometimes has to be done for the health of the overall group. The offending person should be first spoken to in private. If that meeting does not result in changed behavior, then he should be confronted by multiple members of the group. Only after these efforts, should he be asked to leave the group. (This is the process Jesus gave His disciples in Matthew 18:15–17.) It would be wise to include a pastor or church staff member early in this process.

Almost nothing is more toxic to the health of a small group than gossip. It is a prideful sin that should be confronted early and biblically.

Summer and Holidays

The busy summer and holiday seasons can be brutal for new groups, but they don't have to be. With some planning, those busy months can be bonding opportunities and a lot of fun! A few types of groups, like young professionals, may not struggle as much with distractions from summer vacations. They have the luxury of taking vacations when most families with kids in school are not. But groups with families will need to plan ahead to not only survive, but thrive as a group during June and July.

The summer is a perfect time to break from meeting weekly, but continue meeting as a group. Here are four things you can do to stay connected during the summer months:

Hang out together. Go to a ball game. Enjoy the Fourth of July fireworks together. Get together for a picnic. Race cars at an amusement park. Create memories with your group through just hanging out together.

Go on a short-term missions trip. Nothing bonds a group faster than being on mission together. The trip does not have to be international—there are massive needs in communities all around you. Partner with an organization that is already making a difference in that community and take your group on a weekend missions trip.

Serve a local missions organization. There are food pantries, youth centers, and other missional organizations in almost every community. Pick out a Saturday in June or July to serve as a group. If it's a great experience with an organization making a real difference, commit to an ongoing relationship.

Do an online study together. Although you may not be meeting weekly for a study, you can still stay connected by doing an online study.

Just like the summer can be a fun and bonding time for your group, so can the holidays. Here are five things your group can do over the holiday months to maximize the opportunities:

Use an October group meeting to have a pumpkin carving contest. One of our groups started this tradition a few years ago, and it was a huge hit. Just have every person (or couple) bring a pumpkin and a few carving utensils. We would always buy a few extra pumpkins in case someone new was invited that night. My favorite winner was a dead-on version of Walter White from the television show *Breaking Bad.*

Plan a pre-Thanksgiving alternative meal. Everyone loves to eat, and what could be better than a Mexican-themed Thanksgiving meal? Switch up the menu—they'll get plenty of traditional turkey and cranberry sauce on Thanksgiving day.

Serve together at a homeless shelter or ministry on Thanksgiving morning. There are multiple opportunities around cities to serve on Thanksgiving day. You can be finished by mid-morning and ready for your family celebration by 1:00 p.m. Nothing prepares your heart for being thankful more than serving as a group for those without.

Plan an early December Christmas party and then take a break. Most parties don't get started until the second week of December, so prepare your group early to get their ugly sweaters washed before December 1st! Don't worry about trying to have weekly group meetings through the rest of December. The normal rhythm of work and school parties will soon wipe out everyone's calendars.

Get your first meeting in January on the calendar. Instead of scrambling to put something together in the whirlwind of the new year, pick the date early so everyone can be ready for it after the festivities and relatives have disappeared. If you haven't already picked your study for the new year, do that before your last meeting in December. This will give everyone something to look forward to coming back for in January.

With a little planning and creativity, you can make the summer and holidays work for your group, not against it.

My Experience

Summer and holidays can look different when your small group is considered friends and family instead of just members of a group. I want to spend time with friends during those seasons. We may not choose to meet every week for a study, but I don't need a break from my friends for a few months. That mind-set helps me stay excited about our group even when the schedule is inconsistent.

QUESTIONS TO THINK ABOUT

1. What stood out the most to you from this chapter?

_____

_____

2. Which "group killer" sticks out the most to you? Are there any others you would add?

_____

_____

3. Have you experienced the toxicity of gossip? How will you deal with it in your group when it arises?

_____

_____

4. How will your group handle the holidays?

_____

_____

Conclusion

T here will be times when you want to give up. I can say that with a wealth of experience from leading groups for almost twenty years. While leading a small group can be an exhilarating experience—watching people take their next-spiritual steps, seeing prayers answered, celebrating goals achieved—there will also be times of exhaustion and seeming failure. A group member may fall back into a sinful pattern in their life. Others will drop off the radar for no reason. Personal struggles will cause you to question your leadership ability and calling.

In times like these, I dwell on Paul's words to the church in Galatia: "Let us not get tired of doing good, for we will reap at the proper time if we don't give up" (Gal. 6:9). It will sometimes feel like those seasons of drought will last forever, like all the sowing we're doing in the group is coming back void. But as Paul said, the key to reaping the harvest is never giving up.

- If the first group you start doesn't get off the ground, tweak your approach and start another one.
- If the person you approach to be a secondary leader turns you down, be patient and persistent until they are ready, or someone else becomes clear.
- If the group doesn't grow right away, be thankful for who God has sent and pour your heart into them.
- If a group member intentionally or unintentionally wounds you as a leader, seek to understand the cause of their personal pain and work toward healing together.

Too many times we throw in the towel just before a breakthrough. God is using those times of frustration to grow us as disciples. If you persevere and don't quit when things are not going the way you planned, you will be a better leader on the other side.

> Too many times we throw in the towel just before a breakthrough.

In the Bible, Nehemiah faced one of these moments. The people he was leading were halfway through rebuilding the wall of Jerusalem, and they began to get discouraged at the work left in front of them.

In Judah, it was said:
The strength of the laborer fails,
since there is so much rubble.
We will never be able
to rebuild the wall. (Neh. 4:10)

They were having trouble seeing the future of the new wall because of the amount of rubble from the fallen wall. Disappointments in your small group will start to feel like the rubble of fallen potential. Nehemiah pressed on through disappointments, discouragement, and attacks from enemies to finish the wall and create a new future for God's people.

By finishing the task in front of you as a small group leader, you are helping create a new future for the people God has put in your care. Generations of disciples are being created through your group.

Don't give up. Your small group will change the world.

QUESTIONS TO THINK ABOUT

1. What experiences have you had that were so hard you wanted to give up? What helped you push through to the other side?

_____

_____

2. Do you feel ready now as a leader? What next steps do you need to take to be more prepared for your small group?

_____

_____

Resources Appendix

Sample Small Group Covenant

It is important that your group agree on a covenant. Setting these guidelines is the first step toward real Christian community.

We will meet on _____ at _____ o'clock for ____ weeks.

Childcare will be provided by _____.

Food will be _____.

WE AGREE TO . . .

DISCIPLESHIP

- Make our meetings a priority
- Have Bible study at least three times per month
- Pray for the lost

- Worship personally in quiet time and corporately
- Develop future leaders
- Allow everyone to participate in discussion
- Challenge each other on our path to growing to be like Christ

COMMUNITY

- Host monthly socials and quarterly outreach events
- Allow group members to hold us accountable to the commitments we make
- Share the workload of small group
- Call on each other at any time
- Respect each other's opinions
- Keep discussions confidential unless permission is granted
- Have fun!

SERVICE

- Encourage members to serve each other as needed
- Serve God through on-campus opportunities of our church

- Serve the world by praying, encouraging people to go, and/or supporting participants of mission experiences
- Serve the community by identifying a project, whether monthly or annually or on-going, that our group will adopt

Signed: _____

Sample Icebreakers

Icebreakers help everyone in the group feel more comfortable about entering the discussion before the Bible study starts. Try these at your first meetings.

I Know Who You Are

This is a twist on the Two Truths and a Lie game.

1. Give each person two pieces of paper and a pen or pencil.
2. Have each participant write their name and three facts about themselves on one paper—the facts must be true but should be obscure and probably not known by the other group members.

3. Direct the participants to number the other paper with one number for each person present.

4. The leader collects the papers and reads aloud the facts on each sheet, keeping track of the names that match the facts read.

5. The participants write their guesses next to the numbers on their sheets.

6. Once everyone has completed their sheet of numbers and name guesses, read aloud the answers and see who had the most correct to determine a winner.

This Tells about Me

This icebreaker will help new group members get to know each other a little better.

1. Have each person pull out a personal item from his or her purse or pocket, or use an item of clothing or an accessory he or she is wearing.

2. Go around the circle, with each person telling something about them as it relates to the item they have chosen. For example, a person may choose a

wallet-sized picture of their husband and share how they met, or a comb and explain that they are a hairstylist.

Play-Dough Personality

This icebreaker allows the group members to show their creative side.

1. Have everyone sit at a table or provide a surface (such as trays) for this activity.
2. Give each person a reasonable amount of play dough and instruct him or her to make something out of it that represents or describes his or her personality.
3. After small group members are finished, have them take turns sharing their creation and telling the group about it.

Get-to-Know-You Questions

- What do you do for fun?
- What would be your ideal vacation?
- What superhero did you want to be, and why?

- What is the most memorable activity you did with your family as a child?
- What quality do you appreciate most in a friend?
- What is a good thing happening in your life right now? What makes it good?
- If you knew you couldn't fail and money was no object, what would you like to do in the next five years?
- What would you like said at your funeral?

Curriculum Plan Sample

Every pathway has signposts—markers to slow a person's progress on the pathway. LifeWay Research has identified eight signposts of discipleship. These are lifestyle patters that ought to be growing in ever-increasing measure the longer a person walks the pathway of discipleship.

By choosing a study from each of the following categories (signposts) over the course of a year, you will ensure your group is taking a balanced approach to attaining spiritual maturity.

Balanced Discipleship

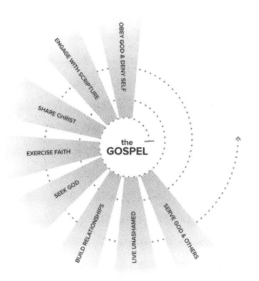

**Obeying God &
Denying Self**
The Apostles' Creed
*What Jesus Demands
    from the World*
Unanswered

**Engage with
Scripture**
*Matthew: The Life of a
    Disciple*
*Genesis: The Life of
    Abraham*
Making Space

**Serving God &
Others**
The Beginning
Experiencing God
Momentum

Seek God
Detours
Religious Liberty
Think Differently

Exercise Faith
Follow Me
*Bible Studies for
    Life: Identity*
*The Mind of
    Christ*

Share Christ
The Mission
Follow Me
Engage

**Build
Relationships**
The Church
Connected
Horizontal Jesus

Live Unashamed
*The Insanity of
    Obedience*
*Jesus Among
    Secular Gods*
Tell Someone

Learn more at LifeWay.com/BalancedDiscipleship.

Childcare Ideas

- Each family makes their own arrangements for child care.
- The group pitches in to hire a babysitter to come to the house where the meeting is or to a nearby house. Each family contributes five to ten dollars per child toward the cost of the sitter.
- Work with the student ministry to hire female babysitters who are raising money for a summer missions trip.
- Work out a co-op relationship with another group that meets on another night.
- Make one night a month a game night where the kids are invited to participate.
- Have one meeting a month where the discussion revolves around a current focus in the church's kids ministry and invite the kids to be a part of the discussion that night.

Sample Small Group Leader Job Description

A job description will help you as the leader understand what the responsibilities and wins are for the small group. You can also use this as you begin to train your secondary leader.

Small Group Leader

OVERVIEW

Small groups are the church's way of making disciples that learn and live the gospel, share the gospel in the community where the small group meets and beyond, and lives in biblical community with one another. In order for people to begin a relationship with Jesus and grow to maturity, every small group must strive to be a gospel-centered community of believers.

RESPONSIBILITIES

Below are the key responsibilities that will enable you to succeed as a small group leader:

- Lead and shepherd a small group of twelve to sixteen adults or less.
- Mentor a secondary leader who will someday lead a small group of their own.
- Pray consistently for the members of the small group you lead.

- Model Christlikeness for the members of the small group you lead.
- Aid group members in learning the gospel and living the gospel.
- Attend all training opportunities (unless something of great importance interferes) offered to small group leaders.
- Share leadership by recruiting members to take on various small group roles (e.g., missional activities, administration, communication, facilitating, prayer time).
- Teach and espouse only those doctrines that align with the church's teachings and doctrines.
- Guide the small group away from discussing controversial church matters during group gatherings.

AUTHORITY AND ACCOUNTABILITY

A small group leader will report to the coach they've been assigned as well as the small group pastor.

The Win

Here would be some examples of a "win" for a small group leader:

- An unbeliever starts attending the small group.
- A small group member comes to know Christ as his Savior and Lord.
- A small group multiplies.
- A small group leader engages in missional and evangelistic living.
- The small group leader trains a future small group leader.
- The small group leader is strategic in discipling those they lead.

Sample Spiritual Gifts List

It's important that group members discover their spiritual gifts as they begin to take ownership in the group. You can find free spiritual gifts tests online to direct members to. Here is a partial list of spiritual gifts and corresponding biblical references, as well as a sample sign-up sheet for areas based on those gifts.

Administration: Luke 14:28–30; Acts 6:1–7; 1 Corinthians 12:28

Craftsmanship: Exodus 31:1–11;
2 Chronicles 34:9–13; Acts 18:2–3

Discernment: Matthew 16:21–23; Acts
5:1–11; 16:16–18; 1 Corinthians 12:10;
1 John 4:1–6

Evangelism: Acts 8:5–6, 26–40; 14:21;
21:8; Ephesians 4:11–14

Exhortation: Acts 14:22; Romans 12:8;
1 Timothy 4:13; Hebrews 10:24–25

Faith: Acts 11:22–24; Romans 4:18–21;
1 Corinthians 12:9; Hebrews 11

Giving: Mark 12:41–44; Romans 12:8;
2 Corinthians 8:1–7; 9:2–7

Healing: Acts 3:1–10; 9:32–35; 28:7–10;
1 Corinthians 12:9, 28

Helps: Mark 15:40–41; Acts 9:36;
Romans 16:1–2; 1 Corinthians 12:28

Intercession: Hebrews 7:25; Colossians
1:9–12; 4:12–13; James 5:14–16

Word of Knowledge: Acts 5:1–11;
1 Corinthians 12:8; Colossians 2:2–3

Leadership: Romans 12:8; 1 Timothy
   3:1–13; 5:17; Hebrews 13:17

Mercy: Matthew 9:35–36; Mark 9:41;
   Romans 12:8; 1 Thessalonians 5:14

Pastor/Shepherd: John 10:1–18;
   Ephesians 4:11–14; 1 Timothy 3:1–7;
   1 Peter 5:1–3

Service: Acts 6:1–7; Romans 12:7;
   Galatians 6:10; Titus 3:14

Teaching: Acts 18:24–28; 20:20–21;
   1 Corinthians 12:28; Ephesians
   4:11–14

Word of Wisdom: Acts 6:3, 10;
   1 Corinthians 2:6–13; 12:8

Sample Small Group Ownership by Gifts Sign-Up Sheet

Name	Communications (Administration, Helps, Service)	Food (Administration, Helps, Service)	Prayer (Faith, Intercession, Healing)	Missional (Evangelism, Craftsmanship, Mercy, Service)	Facilitation (Teaching, Shepherd, Leadership)	Activities (Service, Intercession, Leadership, Administration)
Group Member	X					
Group Member		X				

Sample Small Group Roster and Attendance Sheets

Small Group Attendee Contact Info | Name of Small Group: _____

Name	Address (Street, City, State, Zip)	Phone Number	Email

6-Week Attendance Sheet

Name	Week 1	Week 2	Week 3	Week 4	Week 5	Week 6

Sample Meeting Schedule Time Line

A good length of time for a small group meeting is 1½ to 2 hours. The following schedule gives time at the beginning and end for food and casual conversations.

6:00—Group meeting start time

6:05—Opening prayer and food

6:25—Announcement for moving into the discussion time

6:30—Icebreaker question

6:40—Teaching video

6:55—Bible study discussion

7:30—Prayer time

7:40—Dismiss to finish food and drinks

8:00—Group meeting concludes

Notes

1. C. S. Lewis, *The Four Loves* (New York, NY: Houghton Mifflin Harcourt, 1971), 65.

2. Simon Sinek, *Leaders Eat Last: Why Some Teams Pull Together and Others Don't* (New York, NY: Penguin, 2014, 2017), vii.

3. Timothy Keller, *Preaching: Communicating Faith in an Age of Skepticism* (New York, NY: Penguin Books, 2015), 22.

4. Ibid., 15.

5. http://bfmindia.blogspot.com/2013/03/test-your-spiritual-maturity-by-j.html

6. Peter Scazzero, *Emotionally Healthy Spirituality: Unleash a Revolution in Your Life in Christ* (Nashville, TN: Thomas Nelson, 2011).

7. Joseph Myers, *Organic Community: Creating a Place Where People Naturally Connect* (Grand Rapids, MI: Baker, 2007).

About the Author

Chris Surratt is a ministry consultant and coach with more than twenty years of experience serving the local church. Chris served on the executive teams at Cross Point Church in Nashville, Tennessee, and Seacoast Church in Charleston, South Carolina, prior to becoming the Discipleship and Small Groups Specialist for LifeWay Christian Resources. He is the author of *Small Groups for the Rest of Us: How to Design Your Small Groups System to Reach the Fringes*. You can follow his blog at www.chrissurratt.com.